The
LIES
WE
BELIEVE
WORKBOOK

A COMPREHENSIVE PROGRAM FOR RENEWING

YOUR MIND AND TRANSFORMING YOUR LIFE

DR. CHRIS THURMAN

THOMAS NELSON
Since 1798

The Lies We Believe Workbook

© 2019 by Dr. Chris Thurman

Published in Nashville, Tennessee, by Thomas Nelson. Thomas Nelson is a registered trademark of HarperCollins Christian Publishing, Inc.

Thomas Nelson titles may be purchased in bulk for educational, business, fundraising, or sales promotional use. For information, please e-mail SpecialMarkets@ThomasNelson.com.

ISBN 978-0-310-11214-3 (softcover)

ISBN 978-0-310-11213-6 (epub)

First Printing June 2019 / Printed in the United States of America

Do not merely listen to the word,
and so deceive yourselves.
Do what it says.

JAMES 1:22

CONTENTS

PART FOUR: The Truth Will Set You Free

INTRODUCTION

When I was a kid, my friends and I would dare one another to do things we were afraid to do. I remember being dared once to slip under a chain-link fence into a restricted area on an Air Force base where we lived. My friends and I were certain nuclear bombs were being kept there, and if we could get into the area unnoticed, we might get a peek at them. As young boys, it never occurred to us that given there were no military police posted in the area, the presence of nuclear weapons was unlikely. Nevertheless, with great fear and trembling, I crawled under the fence, sprinted up to the building, saw nothing of importance, and shot like a bullet back under the fence, certain the military police were going to arrest me and kick my dad out of the Air Force because he couldn't keep his wayward son under control.

I tell you this story because I'm going to dare you to do something that might be just as scary for you. I dare you to complete *The Lies We Believe Workbook*. I'm daring you because one of the scariest things we adults face in life is the truth. It takes courage to tackle the truth instead of run from it. So, I'm daring you to do this workbook because facing the truth is scary—something you probably wouldn't do unless someone like me dared you.

The Lies We Believe Workbook is designed to be used with *The Lies We Believe*. For every chapter in the book, there is a corresponding lesson in this workbook to help you put what you've learned into action. As human beings, we are prone to acquire knowledge but not put that knowledge into practical use so we can actually grow from what we learn. Consequently, we fall short of the biblical challenge, "Do not merely listen to the word, and so deceive yourselves. *Do what it says*" (James 1:22, emphasis added).

I encourage you to avoid playing into the enemy's hands by merely reading or listening to the words of *The Lies We Believe*. Instead, lesson by lesson, I want you to take what you learn and put it into action.

In *The Lies We Believe*, I discuss thirty-one ways we falsely view reality across six categories (the lies we believe about ourselves, about others, about life, about God, and about ourselves as men and women). In this workbook, I am going to suggest some additional lies we believe across those categories for you to consider—some of which you may not agree are wrong ways of thinking. You and I don't have to see eye-to-eye on what beliefs qualify as a lie, but I want to offer you more to think about when assessing your beliefs so you can be more self-aware of the faulty "tapes" that are playing inside your mind every day.

In the book, I also discuss twelve of the most important truths we can have for living an emotionally and relationally healthy life. While there are many more truths available, I won't offer any additional possibilities in this workbook (maybe that will be left to another book). Since the Bible says to think on "whatever is true . . . noble . . . right . . . pure . . . lovely . . . admirable" (Philippians 4:8), this workbook is designed to help you do just that. I want you to spend time meditatively thinking about the truth throughout this workbook—and make sure you put as much of that truth into action as possible in how you conduct yourself. Remember, be a *doer* of the truth, and not just a *hearer*.

There are two ways to work through this material. You can read through *The Lies We Believe* and then do the workbook afterward, or you can read a chapter in the book and do the corresponding lesson in the workbook at the same time. Whichever way you decide, be prepared to put on your work gloves. You are going to be working diligently over an extended period of time on thinking more deeply and acting more decisively on the things that are true so you can have a more accurate view of reality and be transformed in the process. Or, to put it a different way, you are going to be thinking more like Christ so you can be more like Christ.

One of the most important issues in becoming a healthy Christian is to learn to see reality the way Christ saw it—free from falsehood or distortion. The emphasis on "What would Jesus do?" is all well and good, but the emphasis in *The Lies We Believe* and this workbook is on "What would Jesus think?" His view of reality was completely true, right, and admirable, and He never felt or acted in a way that was the least bit off the mark of emotional, relational, moral, or spiritual perfection. Christ was the greatest thinker of all time, and no one else comes close in terms of seeing reality exactly as it is and living life in a healthy and loving manner. *No one.* His view of reality will never lead you down the wrong path.

The renewal of your mind is a lifelong process, and we all have to be patient in working out our mental salvation over time. So don't get discouraged as you do the work of renewing your mind. The lies you believe didn't get there overnight, and they aren't going away overnight. Also, while you can read the book and complete this workbook by yourself, I urge you to find others to join you in this effort so that when you grow weary—and you *will* grow weary—you can pick each other up and challenge each other to complete the journey.

In this workbook, I emphasize self-assessment, self-examination, and self-expression, which requires a lot of personal interaction. You'll quickly discover that you enjoy certain types of assignments better than others, but try to give equal importance to all of them. The workbook will only be as helpful as you make it. Give yourself permission to open up freely—perhaps interacting with aspects of your life you've previously kept hidden. Remember, no one is looking over your shoulder, no one is critiquing you, and no one is giving you a grade.

Are you willing to turn your mind over to God and allow Him to renew it with the truth? Are you willing to allow God to help you get better at taking thoughts captive, pulling down toxic mental strongholds, and building truthful strongholds in their place? If you are, I believe God can do some amazing things to help you experience the abundant life.

PART ONE

YOUR BELIEFS
MAKE OR
BREAK YOU

LESSON 1

OUR MINDS ARE UNDER ATTACK

As we first turned away from God in our thoughts, so it is in our thoughts that the first movements toward the renovation of the heart occur. Thoughts are the place where we can and must begin to change.

DALLAS WILLARD

Do not conform to the pattern of this world, but be transformed by the renewing of your mind.

ROMANS 12:2

Our ability to think accurately shattered when the fall of humankind took place. Prior to this event, the first man and woman saw reality as it truly was and lived the way God designed them to live—abundantly. After the fall, their minds distorted everything they experienced, and their lives fell into ruin. They now ran from God rather than enjoy His presence. They blamed others for their actions rather than own their own choices. They adopted a debilitating sense of shame rather than being "naked and unashamed." The catastrophic impact of the fall has rippled through history, and our minds, emotions, and actions haven't been right since.

We don't need to beat ourselves up about the fact that our view of reality is broken. It's not our fault that we came into the world with an impaired capacity to accurately view reality, or that we were raised by parents whose view of reality was flawed, or that we were taught things in church that don't totally square with the truth. We have a spiritual enemy who is *very* good at getting us to believe things that are untrue, and our time on this planet is a constant uphill battle for our minds. But the battle itself is not our fault. What God *does* hold us responsible for is what we are doing to renew our minds and overcome our faulty beliefs. If we are not putting enough effort into overcoming the lies we believe, that's on us.

The apostle Paul said, "When I was a child, I talked like a child, I *thought* like a child, I *reasoned* like a child. When I became a man, I put the ways of childhood behind me" (1 Corinthians 13:11, emphasis added). This is one of the most important challenges facing those who have been spiritually reborn and are now followers of Christ: to go from thinking and acting like a "child" to thinking and acting like a full-fledged adult. Only by putting childish (distorted, faulty, unbiblical) ways of viewing reality behind us can we grow into the kinds of people God meant us to be—loving, gracious, kind, sacrificial, giving, and self-controlled.

In this lesson, I want you to spend some time assessing the beliefs you have about reality. I will tell you up front the first thirty-one statements are lies and the final twelve are all truths. In responding to each statement, I want you to take a minute to deeply think about how strongly you believe/disbelieve that particular way of looking at reality. Don't answer in terms of knowing that something is a lie or truth—answer how you really think. The best way you can do this is by looking at how you actually live your life.

Let me give you an example. One of the lies you are going to respond to is, "My worth is determined by how I perform." You may know in your head this is untrue and thus respond with a *1* (strongly disagree). But if you honestly look at your life, you might have to admit that when you perform badly you feel pretty worthless. For this reason, you should probably answer with a *5* or *6*, indicating you actually strongly agree with a statement you know to be a lie.

In the same way, one of the truths you are going to respond to is, "To err is human." Again, you may know in your head this is true and answer with a *6* or *7*. But if you honestly look at how you live your life, you might have to admit that you beat yourself up for making even the slightest mistake. If that's true, you should probably answer with a *2* or *3*, indicating the deeper belief you have that to make mistakes is not "human."

I'm going into great depth here because the last thing I want you to do is fill out this self-assessment by trying to give the right answer. Please don't do that. Answer each statement honestly in terms of how you actually view reality given your day-to-day actions. Also, don't speed through this self-assessment. Take time to consider each statement and mull over what it is trying to get at. Give each statement at least thirty seconds of contemplation before you answer. As I mentioned in the Introduction, it is important for you to be completely honest with yourself throughout the workbook and "keep it real."

Assessing Your Beliefs

Complete the self-assessment inventory using the scale below. Be honest in terms of how you *actually think* and avoid responding in terms of how you *should think*. Also try to avoid using the neutral response (4). Take time to consider each statement and ask the Holy Spirit to help you see the degree to which you honestly agree or disagree with what it says.

1	2	3	4	5	6	7
Strongly Disagree			Neutral			Strongly Agree

____   1. It's not okay to be human and make mistakes.

____   2. My worth is determined by how I perform.

____   3. I must have everyone's love and approval.

____   4. It is easier to avoid my problems than to face them.

____   5. My unhappiness is externally caused.

____   6. People can meet all my emotional needs.

____   7. Others should accept me just the way I am.

____   8. To get along, everyone needs to think, feel, and act the same way.

____   9. Others are more messed up than me.

____   10. People who hurt me have to earn my forgiveness.

____   11. You can have it all.

____   12. You shouldn't have to wait for what you want.

____   13. You can do anything you set your mind to.

____   14. Being happy is the most important thing in life.

____   15. People are basically good.

_____   16. Life should be easy and fair.

_____   17. God's love must be earned.

_____   18. God is mean and vindictive.

_____   19. God ignores our disobedience.

_____   20. God gives us whatever we want.

_____   21. God has lost control of everything.

_____   22. (Men only): I don't have what it takes to be a man.

_____   23. (Men only): It's not okay to feel sad, scared, or hurt.

_____   24. (Men only): My good intentions ought to satisfy everyone.

_____   25. (Men only): Sex is about my pleasure and enjoyment.

_____   26. (Men only): I can do it by myself.

_____   27. (Women only): My main job in life is to make everyone happy.

_____   28. (Women only): It's not okay to speak my mind.

_____   29. (Women only): I'm facing my flaws.

_____   30. (Women only): I'm not worthy of being loved for who I am.

_____   31. (Women only): Outer beauty is more important than inner beauty.

Add your responses and divide by 26 (remember, you aren't supposed to respond to the lies the opposite sex believes). This is the average degree to which you agree or disagree with these faulty statements (lies). Next, look through the answers and circle the statements you gave a *5*, *6*, or *7*, as these responses suggest you agree with a faulty way of thinking. Finally, look at the statements you gave a *6* or *7* and pick three beliefs you struggle with the most. These are the lies to pay the most attention to as you work on renewing your mind.

Continue by completing the self-assessment inventory on the next page using the same scale. Again, respond in terms of how you *actually think* and avoid responding in terms of how you *should think*. Try to avoid using the neutral response (*4*), mull over each statement in your mind, and ask the Holy Spirit to help you see the degree to which you agree or disagree with what it says. Avoid the temptation to respond to these statements "correctly" and instead answer in terms of how your actions in day-to-day life reveal the way you really think.

1	2	3	4	5	6	7
Strongly Disagree			Neutral			Strongly Agree

_____ 1. To err is human.

_____ 2. You can't please everyone.

_____ 3. There's no gain without pain.

_____ 4. Love never fails.

_____ 5. It's not all about you.

_____ 6. Life is difficult.

_____ 7. Accept what you can't change, change what you can.

_____ 8. It is more blessed to give than to receive.

_____ 9. You are a person of great worth.

_____ 10. The world owes you nothing.

_____ 11. The victory lies in the effort, not the result.

_____ 12. You are going to die.

Add your scores and divide the total by 12. This is the average degree to which you agree or disagree with these truths. Next, look through the answers you gave and circle every statement you gave a *1*, *2*, or *3*, as these items suggest you disagree with a right way of thinking. Finally, pick the three truths you have the hardest time believing. These are the truths to pay the most attention to as you work on renewing your mind.

To cap things off, go back to the first self-assessment and write down the three lies you believe the *most* strongly—the ones that are causing you the most psychological, relational, and spiritual damage.

Lie #1:

_____

_____

_____

Lie #2:

_____

_____

_____

Lie #3:

_____

_____

_____

Now go to the second self-assessment and write down the three truths you believe the *least* strongly—the ones that are affecting your ability to live your life well because you don't believe them.

Truth #1:

_____

_____

_____

Truth #2:

_____

_____

_____

Truth #3:

_____

_____

_____

As you continue to work through the thirty-one lies we will cover in this workbook, and then each of the twelve truths, keep your eye on the three lies you believe the most strongly and the three truths you believe the least strongly. Ask God to help you renew your mind in these six ways so this program can be uniquely tailored to the faulty beliefs you struggle with in life.

Key Memory and Meditation Verses

Buy the truth and do not sell it—wisdom, instruction and insight as well (Proverbs 23:23).

"When he lies, he speaks his native language, for he is a liar and the father of lies" (John 8:44).

"But when he, the Spirit of truth comes, he will guide you into all truth" (John 16:13).

The mind governed by the flesh is death, but the mind governed by the Spirit is life and peace (Romans 8:6).

Do not conform to the pattern of this world, but be transformed by the renewing of your mind (Romans 12:2).

Contemplative Prayer
(to be read slowly, meditatively, and repeatedly)

Heavenly Father,

Thank You that You are truth and that in You there is no hint of falsehood or deception. You ask that I love You with all my heart, mind, soul, and strength, and I ask in return that through the power of the Holy Spirit, You will help me be transformed by the renewal of my mind over the months and years to come.

Father, I know that the enemy is the father of lies, that he is out to kill and steal and destroy me, and that he works tirelessly every day to get me to believe things that are not true. I know that the mind governed by the Spirit is life and peace and that if I turn to You for how to view reality, I will have joy, peace, and contentment that go beyond my circumstances. I know that You want me to be like-minded with my brothers and sisters in Christ, and I ask You to help us be unified in understanding and internalizing the central truths of the Christian faith.

Please, Father, help me to become more disciplined in studying Your Word by meditating on it day and night. Help me to buy the truth and not sell it. Help me to not fall into thinking the way the enemy wants me to think or the way the world I live in would direct me to go. Help me through Your Spirit to be more aware of the lies I believe and take what You say about them to heart each day. You promise the truth will set me free, and I desperately need Your help to believe the truth in my innermost being so I can experience the freedom and abundant life You offer us through Your Son.

In the precious and holy name of Your Son, Jesus Christ. Amen.

LESSON 2

THE HIGH COST OF
THE LIES WE BELIEVE

*The mind is its own place and in itself can make
a Heav'n of Hell, a Hell of Heav'n.*

JOHN MILTON

*The simple believe anything,
but the prudent give thought to their steps.*

PROVERBS 14:15

In the previous lesson, you assessed the degree to which you agree/disagree with thirty-one lies and twelve truths. In agreeing with any of the lies, and in disagreeing with any of the truths, you cause harm to your psychological, relational, and spiritual health. In this lesson, you are going to access the cost of the faulty beliefs you have carried with you through life.

Garbage In, Garbage Out

The faulty beliefs you have adopted will negatively impact you "across the board" in life. The enemy wants you to believe things that are untrue because he knows the lies you believe come with a price tag—diminished functioning and well-being and an inability to experience the abundant life Christ came to offer. Before you begin this lesson, take a minute to go back to the self-assessments you completed in lesson 1 and remind yourself of what your most strongly held lies are and the truths that you believe rather weakly.

Next, in the space provided below, write down how these faulty ways of viewing reality have damaged your life. Go all the way back to childhood if needed, but take a "30,000-foot view" of your life in terms of the negative impact your unbiblical beliefs have had on damaging your emotional, relational, and spiritual health. In each area, I'm going to suggest some possibilities for how faulty beliefs can harm you, but personalize it to the specific ways that "stinking thinking" has been harmful to you.

How the Lies I Believe Have Damaged My View of Me
(I think I'm worthless; I believe I am unworthy of love; I think it is always my fault when I experience conflict; I don't believe it is okay to make mistakes; I struggle to acknowledge the good traits and qualities God created in me.)

_____

_____

_____

_____

_____

_____

_____

How the Lies I Believe Have Damaged My Emotional Health
(I struggle with feeling depressed, anxious, or angry; I feel bitter and resentful at times; I never seem to be happy or peaceful; I experience a fair amount of shame and self-condemnation; I feel more like a "human doing" rather than a human being.)

_____

_____

_____

_____

_____

_____

_____

How the Lies I Believe Have Damaged My Relationships with Others
(I pull away from people and isolate; I am overly dependent on others for how I feel about myself; I treat others in passive-aggressive and/or aggressive ways when I feel hurt; my relationships are short-lived and end painfully; I allow others to take advantage of me.)

_____

_____

_____

_____

_____

_____

_____

How the Lies I Believe Have Damaged My Way of Looking at Life
(I don't see life as having much meaning; I see life as a competition, where there are only winners and losers; I expect life to give me everything I want; I feel like a failure when my dreams don't come true; I don't go out into the world to make things better for others.)

_____

_____

_____

_____

_____

_____

_____

How the Lies I Believe Have Damaged My Relationship with God
(I run from God rather than toward Him; I expect God to give me what I ask for and feel bitter when He doesn't; I blame God for all the bad things that come my way; I feel that God's love depends on how I act each day; I don't find myself thirsting for a deep relationship with God.)

_____

_____

_____

_____

_____

You don't need me to point out the obvious, but I'm going to anyway: the lies we believe are incredibly damaging to how we view ourselves, the quality of our emotional health, our relationship with others, how we go through day-to-day life, and, most importantly, our relationship with God. The father of lies, in his efforts to "kill and steal and destroy," is out to take no prisoners when it comes to keeping us from the quality of life God wants us to have. Sadly, by believing the enemy's lies, we play right into his hands. As C. S. Lewis put it, "We are half-hearted creatures, fooling around with drink, sex, and ambition, when infinite joy is offered us, like an ignorant child who wants to go on making mud pies in a slum because he cannot imagine what is meant by the offer of a holiday at the sea. We are far too easily pleased."[1]

Now, I didn't ask you to assess how the lies you believe have damaged your life so I could rub your nose in it. I did it solely for the purpose of pushing you to be more aware of the cost of faulty thinking and to motivate you to get angry about what the enemy is doing. Like the news anchor in the movie *Network*, you need to say, "I'm as mad as hell, and I'm not going to take this anymore!" You need to ask God to give you the righteous anger Jesus had when He threw the money lenders out of the temple, so you can throw out the lies you believe and prevent them from wreaking further havoc on your life. Don't take it anymore!

Go back and review what you wrote about how your faulty views of reality have damaged your life. If that doesn't fire you up, you have played into what C. S. Lewis is warning about—being too easily pleased with "making mud pies in a slum" because you can't imagine what God is offering with "a holiday at the sea." You've paid way too high a price for the lies you believe. Refuse to accept that kind of life. Clear the temple.

Key Memory and Meditation Verses

An angry person stirs up conflict, and a hot-tempered person commits many sins (Proverbs 29:22).

I denied myself nothing my eyes desired; I refused my heart no pleasure. My heart took delight in all my labor, and this was the reward for my toil. Yet when I surveyed all that my hands had done and what I had toiled to achieve, everything was meaningless, a chasing after the wind; nothing was gained under the sun (Ecclesiastes 2:10–11).

Those who live according to the flesh have their minds set on what the flesh desires; but those who live in accordance with the Spirit have their minds set on what the Spirit desires (Romans 8:5).

The acts of the flesh are obvious: sexual immorality, impurity and debauchery, idolatry and witchcraft; hatred, discord, jealousy, fits of rage, selfish ambition, dissensions, factions and envy; drunkenness, orgies, and the like (Galatians 5:19–21).

Get rid of all bitterness, rage and anger, brawling and slander, along with every form of malice (Ephesians 4:31).

Contemplative Prayer
(to be read slowly, meditatively, and repeatedly)

Heavenly Father,

I have paid such a high and unnecessary price for the lies I believe. They have cost me greater emotional health, close relationships with others, a sense of meaning and purpose in how I'm living my life, less control over my sinful reactions to difficult and painful situations, and, most importantly, a close and intimate relationship with You.

Father, please help me to turn away in my mind from the lies I believe and toward the truth that only comes from You. Help me to quit giving in to the desires of my flesh, to bitterness and resentment toward others, to acting with malice toward people, and to the toxic feelings of shame that have cost me joy, peace, and contentment throughout my life.

Father, I desperately need Your help to turn from my waywardness, to come back to You, and to grow in living life in a mature, Christlike manner. I know You want these things for me and that You are out to help me and not to harm me. Thank You for being my God and for wanting what is best for me.

In the precious and holy name of Your Son, Jesus Christ. Amen.

PULLING DOWN
MENTAL STRONGHOLDS

*As a single footstep will not a path make on the earth, so a
single thought will not make a pathway in the mind. . . .
To make a deep mental path, we must think over and over
the kinds of thoughts we wish to dominate our lives.*

HENRY DAVID THOREAU

*The weapons we fight with are not the weapons
of the world. On the contrary, they have
divine power to demolish strongholds.*

2 CORINTHIANS 10:4

In lesson 1, we explored how important it is to be aware of what we believe (content), how strongly we believe it (certainty), and how important a belief is to our worldview (centrality). We examined how the truth can set us free—but not without hard work on our part. In this lesson, the hard work will begin. I am going to teach you the TRUTH model and encourage you to start using it to become more aware of the lies you believe, the damaging impact of these lies on your life, the truth that you will need to move forward, and how the truth can set you free to experience a psychologically, relationally, and spiritually healthy life.

The TRUTH Model

The TRUTH model is a practical way for you to break down your day-to-day life into five important parts:

T: Trigger Events—external events/situations that trigger a response in you
R: Ruined Thoughts—faulty/unbiblical views (lies) you filter those events through
U: Unhealthy Response—unhealthy emotional/behavioral response toward the event
T: Truthful Thoughts—accurate/biblical view of the situation
H: Healthy Response—healthier emotional/behavioral response to the event

The first *T* of the model, "trigger events," refers to the situations you encounter each day that set you off—external things like someone cutting you off in traffic, your boss criticizing you in front of coworkers, a spouse not giving you much time or attention, or, if you're a parent, your children not obeying you and causing a ruckus. The focus here is on the things that are upsetting, hurtful, and even traumatic—not on the pleasant and uplifting things that happen in life. In the space below, take a minute to write down the kinds of events that happen to you that you find aversive—the events that tend to trigger you feeling upset.

T: Events That Negatively Trigger Me

_____

_____

_____

_____

_____

Now, let's jump past *R* for a moment and talk about *U*. The *U*, "unhealthy response," refers to how you react in what we psychologist-types call a "dysregulated" way to the event that took place. Scripture would refer to *U* as where you respond to aversive events out of the "flesh" and have sinful reactions to the things people do or that life throws your way. This is possibly what the apostle Paul was talking about when he said, "I do not understand what I do. For what I want to do I do not do, but what I hate I do. . . . As it is, it is no longer I myself who do it, but it is sin living in me. For I know that good itself does not dwell in me, that is, in my sinful nature" (Romans 7:15, 17–18). In the space below, take a minute to write down the sinful and dysregulated ways you react to the aversive events that happen to you.

<u>U</u>: Unhealthy Ways I Respond to the Events That Trigger Me

_____

_____

_____

_____

_____

Next, let's go back to the **R**, "ruined thoughts," which refers to how you wrongly perceive, interpret, and assess the things that happen to you. In other words, **R** is where you filter trigger events through the lies you believe. Not to psychobabble here, but your faulty thoughts about the things that happen to you are often *unconscious* and *fast*. Most of the time, you aren't even aware you had any thoughts about the event. Typically, you will just be aware of the emotions you feel about what happened and what action you took as a response. You assessed your faulty "tapes" in lesson 1, and the lies you believe the most strongly are probably the ones you filter a lot of trigger events through. In the space below, write down the lies that you tend to unconsciously and quickly default to when mentally reacting to trigger events.

<u>R</u>: Ruined Thoughts/Lies I Filter Trigger Events Through

_____

_____

_____

_____

_____

The second **T** in the model, "truthful thoughts," refers to what you are *supposed* to filter trigger events through. To say it differently, you are supposed to mentally filter the aversive things that happen to you through the same beliefs, attitudes, and expectations that Christ had when He ran into mistreatment. Go back to the self-assessment you did of the twelve truths you are supposed to believe as you go through life. In the space below, write down the three or four truths you especially need to work on strengthening in your mind so that when bad things happen, these beliefs can increasingly be in control for how you mentally react.

<u>T</u>: Truths I Need to Filter Trigger Events Through

_____

_____

_____

_____

_____

Finally, the **H**, "healthy response," refers to the way you are meant to respond to the trigger events you encounter. If you keep working with God to replace your lies with the truth, you can react to painful circumstances "in the Spirit" and respond to the things that happen to you in a non-sinful, Christlike way. In the space below, write down how you would respond to upsetting or disturbing situations if you filtered them through the truth.

<u>H</u>: Healthy Ways I Can Respond to Trigger Events

_____

_____

_____

_____

_____

I want you to keep a *TRUTH Journal* as you're going through this workbook (see page 32 for an example of the template). You may not be a big fan of journaling, but I want you to get into the habit of writing things down using the TRUTH model so you can better understand the kinds of events that trigger you, the unhealthy reactions you have, the ruined/faulty thoughts that are causing your dysregulated/sinful responses to events, the specific truths you need to keep working on for how you view reality, and how, over time, the truth can help you experience greater spiritual, psychological, and relational health and well-being.

Using a separate notebook, copy the top two rows of the template and then make entries about situations where you experienced a *noticeably strong emotional/behavioral reaction* to an event. Do so in the following order:

(1) In the *U* column, write down what you felt emotionally and the behavior that went along with your feelings.

(2) In the first *T* column, write down what triggered your response.

(3) In the *R* column, write down the "ruined" (faulty, erroneous, irrational, unbiblical, distorted, inaccurate) thoughts that went through your mind.

(4) In the second *T* column, write down what your thoughts would have been if they were true, noble, right, pure, lovely, and admirable.

(5) In the *H* column, write down if there were any *noticeable* changes in your emotional and behavioral reactions to the event, given the right thoughts you ran through your mind.

In all my years as a psychologist, every client who *regularly journaled* using the TRUTH method made noticeable gains not only in their ability to think more biblically but also in handling life in an emotionally and behaviorally healthier manner. So, please, start using the *TRUTH Journal* today. Let God use it to set you free from the toxic thoughts that go through your mind each day and from the unhealthy ways of coping with life that they cause. The truth will set you free, but you have to do the hard work on your end to make that happen.

To help all this sink in, let me share some examples of situations my clients encountered and how they ran them through the TRUTH model. Just a quick reminder: always start with *U* and write down what you felt and how you acted, go to the first *T* and fill in what triggered you, go to *R* and write down your faulty thoughts, go to the second *T* and fill in the right thoughts about the situation, and finish by filling in *H* with any changes—no matter how small—in your feelings and actions toward the event.

Try to keep up with your *TRUTH Journal* every day. Given how deeply embedded our faulty beliefs are about reality, you simply cannot afford to be lukewarm in your efforts to renew your mind. So, please, spend time each day reviewing what happened to you and how you responded to it. The truth really can set you free—but only if you work at it.

T	R	U	T	H
Trigger Event	**Ruined Thoughts**	**Unhealthy Response**	**Truthful Thoughts**	**Healthy Response**
Lost my car keys and missed an important meeting at work.	*I'm such an idiot. Why do I always do stupid things like this! Why can't I ever get my act together!*	Got angry and threw my phone across the room.	*I'm not an idiot. I don't do this kind of thing very often, and I need to cut myself some slack for being a human being.*	Felt less angry, picked up my phone, and called my boss to let her know I was going to be late.
Teenage son talked down to me in front of his girlfriend and a couple of his friends.	*I deserve to be treated better than that. He owes me an apology!*	Felt bitter and said, "I'll be glad when you go off to college!"	*It's not okay for my son to talk to me like that, but it's not okay for me to talk to him that way either.*	Calmed down, apologized to my son, asked him to forgive me, and suggested that we both keep trying to talk to each other respectfully.
Friend forgot we were supposed have lunch today.	*I can't depend on him—I've got nothing but losers for friends!*	Felt angry and left him a snarky voicemail.	*He makes mistakes like everyone else. He's a good friend, and I'm thankful he's my friend.*	Felt less angry, called back to say I was sorry for the snarky voicemail, and rescheduled our lunch.

Whenever you undertake a difficult challenge like this, ask God to empower your efforts. As the psalmist wrote, "Unless the Lord builds the house, the builders labor in vain" (Psalm 127:1). We can't afford to try to build our mental house by relying on our own power. Our fallen and finite minds can't fix our fallen and finite minds—we have to ask God to help us. The Holy Spirit plays a number of roles in our lives, but some of the most important are related to how He teaches us and helps us remember the things we learn about God (see John 14:26), convicts us of sin (see John 16:8), gives us strength to resist sin (see Galatians 5:16), helps us pray (see Romans 8:26), reveals the deep things of God (see 1 Corinthians 2:10), and guides us to truth (see John 16:13). So make sure you ask God to help you each step of the way.

Key Memory and Meditation Verses

Give careful thought to the paths for your feet and be steadfast in all your ways (Proverbs 4:26).

The mind governed by the flesh is death, but the mind governed by the Spirit is life and peace (Romans 8:6).

Do not conform to the pattern of this world, but be transformed by the renewing of your mind (Romans 12:2).

We demolish arguments and every pretension that sets itself up against the knowledge of God, and we take captive every thought to make it obedient to Christ (2 Corinthians 10:5).

You were taught, with regard to your former way of life, to put off your old self, which is being corrupted by its deceitful desires; to be made new in the attitude of your minds (Ephesians 4:22–23).

Finally, brothers and sisters, whatever is true, whatever is noble, whatever is right, whatever is pure, whatever is lovely, whatever is admirable—if anything is excellent or praiseworthy—think about such things (Philippians 4:8).

Contemplative Prayer
(to be read slowly, meditatively, and repeatedly)

Heavenly Father,

Your Word is alive and active, penetrating to even dividing soul and spirit. It judges the thoughts and attitudes of the heart and illumines the path ahead of me. You have done Your part by providing Your Word and indwelling me with the Holy Spirit. Now, I pray that You will empower me to do my part by studying Your Word, taking thoughts captive, and dedicating the rest of my life to thinking on what is true, noble, right, pure, lovely, and admirable.

Father, when I was a child I thought and reasoned like a child. I ask for Your help to put childish ways of thinking behind me so my mind would increasingly become the mind of an adult who sees reality the way Jesus did. Thank You for loving me by providing Your Word. Please help me to wash my mind in Your truth each and every day so I can experience the abundant life that Christ came to offer.

In the precious and holy name of Your Son, Jesus Christ. Amen.

PART TWO

THE LIES WE BELIEVE

THE LIES WE BELIEVE
ABOUT OURSELVES

Nothing is so easy as to deceive one's self;
for what we wish, we readily believe.

DEMOSTHENES

Don't be deceived, my dear brothers and sisters.

JAMES 1:16

All of us have ways of thinking about ourselves that are unbiblical and destructive to our psychological, relational, and spiritual health. In this lesson, we will explore some of the most damaging ways we think about ourselves as we go through life. These are only the tip of the iceberg when it comes to the faulty notions we have about ourselves, and they often lead to mood problems, interpersonal conflict, and a watered-down relationship with God.

Assessing Your Beliefs

Complete the following self-assessment inventory of the lies you might believe about yourself using the scale below. Note that I have included some additional lies that were not featured in the accompanying *Lies We Believe* book. As you complete this assessment, it is important for you to be as honest as possible in terms of how you *actually think* about yourself and avoid responding to the items in terms of how you *should think*. Once again, knowing these are all unbiblical ways of thinking about yourself, be honest about whether or not you think in these ways. Try to avoid using the neutral response (*4*) whenever possible.

1	2	3	4	5	6	7
Strongly Disagree			Neutral			Strongly Agree

____ 1. It's not okay to be human and make mistakes.

____ 2. My worth is determined by how I perform.

____ 3. I must have everyone's love and approval.

____ 4. It is easier to avoid my problems than to face them.

____ 5. My unhappiness is externally caused.

____ 6. I can do anything I set my mind to.

____ 7. I'm entitled to love and respect from others.

____ 8. I'm basically a good person.

____ 9. I have a reasonably accurate view of myself.

____ 10. My happiness is the most important thing in life.

____ 11. My sins are unforgivable.

____ 12. My life should be relatively easy and problem-free.

____ 13. I'm unlovable given the flaws and defects I have.

____ 14. If people knew the real me, they would reject me.

____ 15. I can have it all.

Look back through your answers and circle the statements you gave a *5* or higher, as these responses suggest you have a faulty way of thinking about yourself that is causing some degree of damage to your life. Next, we will turn our attention to the *truths* about you and how you can renew your mind with these biblically accurate ways of looking at yourself.

The Truth About You

I have listed below what I consider to be the most important truths you must believe about yourself in order to live life the way God intended. The first four apply to every person on the planet, whether he or she is a follower of Christ or not. The remaining eleven are only true of those who have experienced spiritual rebirth and accepted God's offer to be a part of his family. If you are a Christian, all fifteen truths should reflect the way you think about yourself as you live out your life. In the space provided below, restate each of these truths in your own words and personalize them as best you can. Also write down how you would live differently if you really believed each of these statements to be true about yourself.

Truth #1: You Bear God's Image

So God created mankind in his own image, in the image of God he created them (Genesis 1:27).

_____

_____

_____

_____

_____

_____

_____

Truth #2: You Are Fearfully and Wonderfully Made

For you created my inmost being; you knit me together in my mother's womb. I praise you because I am fearfully and wonderfully made; your works are wonderful, I know that full well (Psalm 139:13–14).

_____

_____

_____

_____

_____

_____

_____

Truth #3: You Are Adam's Offspring and Have a Natural Bent to Sin

Surely I was sinful at birth, sinful from the time my mother conceived me (Psalm 51:5).

_____

_____

_____

_____

_____

_____

_____

Truth #4: You Are of Infinite Value to God

For there is one God and one mediator between God and mankind, the man Christ Jesus, who gave himself as a ransom for all people (1 Timothy 2:5–6).

_____

_____

_____

_____

_____

_____

_____

Truth #5: You Are God's Child

In love he predestined us for adoption to sonship through Jesus Christ, in accordance with his pleasure and will (Ephesians 1:4–5).

_____

_____

_____

_____

_____

_____

Truth #6: You Are a Brother or Sister to Christ

Both the one who makes people holy and those who are made holy are of the same family.
So Jesus is not ashamed to call them brothers and sisters (Hebrews 2:11–12).

_____

_____

_____

_____

_____

_____

_____

Truth #7: You Are a Joint Heir with Christ

So you are no longer a slave, but God's child; and since you are his child, God has also
made you an heir (Galatians 4:7).

_____

_____

_____

_____

_____

_____

_____

Truth #8: You Have the Holy Spirit as a
Guarantee You Belong to God

When you believed, you were marked in him with a seal, the promised Holy Spirit, who
is a deposit guaranteeing our inheritance until the redemption of those who are God's
possession—to the praise of his glory (Ephesians 1:13–14).

_____

_____

_____

_____

_____

_____

Truth #9: You Have Christ's Life Within You

For you died, and your life is now hidden with Christ in God. When Christ, who is your life, appears, then you also will appear with him in glory (Colossians 3:3–4).

_____

_____

_____

_____

_____

_____

_____

Truth #10: You Have Christ's Righteousness Imputed to You

God made him who had no sin to be sin for us, so that in him we might become the righteousness of God (2 Corinthians 5:21).

_____

_____

_____

_____

_____

_____

_____

Truth #11: You Will Never Be Condemned by God

Therefore, there is now no condemnation for those who are in Christ Jesus, because through Christ Jesus the law of the Spirit who gives life has set you free from the law of sin and death (Romans 8:1–2).

_____

_____

_____

_____

_____

_____

_____

Truth #12: You Are a Foreigner in This World

Dear friends, I urge you, as foreigners and exiles, to abstains from sinful desires, which wage war against your soul (1 Peter 2:11).

_____

_____

_____

_____

_____

_____

_____

_____

Truth #13: You Have Special God-Given Gifts

We have different gifts, according to the grace given to each of us (Romans 12:6).

_____

_____

_____

_____

_____

_____

_____

_____

Truth #14: You Are an Ambassador

We are therefore Christ's ambassadors, as though God were making his appeal through us (2 Corinthians 5:20).

_____

_____

_____

_____

_____

_____

_____

_____

Truth #15: You Can Confidently Ask God for Help

Let us then approach God's throne of grace with confidence, so that we may receive mercy and find grace to help us in our time of need (Hebrews 4:16).

_____

_____

_____

_____

_____

_____

_____

_____

Imagine you deeply believed every one of these statements to be true. How would it affect the way you go out into the world each day and conduct yourself? You are a fearfully and wonderfully made image-bearer. You are of infinite value to God. If you have accepted God's offer of salvation, you are His child, a joint heir with Christ, a brother or sister to Christ, and have the Holy Spirit living inside you as a guarantee you belong to God. You have Christ's life in you. His righteousness has been credited to your account. He will never condemn you. You have God-given gifts and abilities, are an ambassador on behalf of Christ, and can confidently ask God for His help.

These are mind-boggling truths! So don't listen to what the father of lies has to say about you and walk around with your head down. Listen to what the One who made you says about you and live with confidence. God will never lie to you about who you are in His eyes.

The TRUTH Model

Review each of the fifteen truths listed above and choose three that speak the most powerfully to you. Use the TRUTH model to journal where these lies you believe about yourself are rearing their ugly heads as well as the biblical truths you can use to move in a more biblically solid direction. Below is an example of how that might look.

The enemy is going to attack you throughout your life on a worth-and-value level, so you need to be ready with the truth about what God says in each of these areas.

Shame and condemnation will be the deadliest weapons he will use against you, so if you have such thoughts, you can know they come from the father of lies. On the other hand, God simply wants you to learn from your mistakes and do better over time, so if your thoughts are that you have worth and value but are a work in progress, you can know those thoughts are from the God who is truth and would never want you to think otherwise.

T	R	U	T	H
Trigger Event	**Ruined Thoughts**	**Unhealthy Response**	**Truthful Thoughts**	**Healthy Response**
Gave a horrible presentation at work to the board of directors.	*I'm worthless and have nothing good to offer at work. I am going to be let go or demoted.*	Felt discouraged and was tempted to quit my job.	*Giving a bad talk at work doesn't mean I don't have a lot to offer. Everyone messes up.*	Felt more upbeat, apologized to my boss, and asked for feedback on how to improve.

Key Memory and Meditation Verses

Memorize the three verses that relate to the truths you selected that spoke the most powerfully to you. Spend some time this week meditating specifically on those verses so God can help you get the most meaning and significance from them as you can.

Contemplative Prayer
(to be read slowly, meditatively, and repeatedly)

> *Heavenly Father,*
> *Thank You for creating me in Your image, fearfully and wonderfully knitting me together in a way that You called "very good." Even though I was born with a fallen bent to sin, You sent Your Son to earth to pay for my sins and bring me back into Your family, making me Your child in the process. Thank You for imputing Your righteousness to me in what Christ did on the cross.*

Thank You, Father, that Christ is not ashamed to call me a brother or sister, for sealing me by indwelling me with the Holy Spirit, and for making me an heir to all Your riches in heaven. You have set me free from being enslaved to sin, empowered me to live in freedom, made me your ambassador here on earth, and removed the barrier between You and me so I can approach Your throne with confidence and find mercy and grace in my time of need.

I will never be able to thank You enough for all that You have done to express Your pure, undefiled love for me. Today, I ask for Your help to spend the rest of my life serving at Your pleasure.

In the precious and holy name of Your Son, Jesus Christ, Amen.

THE LIES WE BELIEVE ABOUT OTHERS

*Whenever you're in conflict with someone, there is one
factor that can make the difference between damaging your
relationship and deepening it. That factor is your attitude.*

WILLIAM JAMES

*Give careful thought to the paths for your feet
and be steadfast in all your ways.*

PROVERBS 4:26

Not only do we believe lies about ourselves, but we also believe lies about others. However inaccurately we look at who we are as individuals before God, we look at others just as inaccurately. As a result, we don't treat other people well at times. Not only do we need God's help to see ourselves clearly, but we also need His help to see others clearly so we will treat them the way Christ did—kindly, caringly, and graciously. In this lesson, we will examine some of the most destructive ways we look at others. As in the previous lesson, there are some additional lies we believe about others not included in the book for you to consider.

Assessing Your Beliefs

Begin by completing the following self-assessment inventory using the scale below. Even though you know these are all faulty ways of thinking about others, be as honest as you can about the degree to which you agree or disagree with each statement. Again, try to avoid using the neutral response (*4*) as much as possible.

1	2	3	4	5	6	7
Strongly Disagree			Neutral			Strongly Agree

_____ 1. People can meet all of my needs.

_____ 2. Others should accept me just the way I am.

_____ 3. To get along, everyone needs to think, feel, and act the same way.

_____ 4. Others are more messed up than me.

_____ 5. People who hurt me have to earn my forgiveness.

_____ 6. People can't be trusted.

_____ 7. Others have more worth and value than me.

_____ 8. People are basically good.

_____ 9. Everyone else has their act more together than me.

_____ 10. People sometimes do things that just can't be forgiven.

_____ 11. If others don't think like I do, they're the ones who are wrong.

_____ 12. People only think about themselves.

_____ 13. If others do something kind, they always want something in return.

_____ 14. Everyone is more gifted and talented than me.

_____ 15. Some people have it all.

Look back through your answers and circle the statements you gave a *5* or higher, as these responses suggest you have a faulty way of thinking about others that is causing some degree of damage to your life. Next, we will turn our attention to the *truths* about others and how you can renew your mind with these biblically accurate ways of looking at people.

The Truth About People

I have listed below what I consider to be the most important truths about others that are essential for you to believe if you are going to treat people properly as you go through life. (Note that you explored some of these truths in the previous lesson.) Write down your thoughts about each of these statements as to whether or not you see people this way.

Truth #1: People Bear the Image of God
So God created mankind in his own image, in the image of God he created them (Genesis 1:27).

_____

_____

_____

_____

_____

_____

_____

_____

_____

Truth #2: People Are Fearfully and Wonderfully Made
For you created my inmost being; you knit me together in my mother's womb. I praise you because I am fearfully and wonderfully made; your works are wonderful, I know that full well (Psalm 139:13–14).

_____

_____

_____

_____

_____

_____

_____

_____

Truth #3: People Are Adam's Offspring and Have a Natural Bent to Sin

Surely I was sinful at birth, sinful from the time my mother conceived me (Psalm 51:5).

_____

_____

_____

_____

_____

_____

_____

_____

Truth #4: People Are of Infinite Value to God

For there is one God and one mediator between God and mankind, the man Christ Jesus, who gave himself as a ransom for all people (1 Timothy 2:5–6).

_____

_____

_____

_____

_____

_____

_____

_____

Truth #5: People Can Meet Some of Our Needs Some of the Time

My God will meet all your needs according to the riches of his glory in Christ Jesus (Philippians 4:19).

_____

_____

_____

_____

_____

_____

_____

_____

**Truth #6: People Need to Accept Each Other
but Challenge One Another to Grow**

As iron sharpens iron, so one person sharpens another (Proverbs 27:17).

_____

_____

_____

_____

_____

_____

_____

Truth #7: People Are God's Masterpieces and Designed to Be Unique

*You have searched me, LORD, and you know me. You know when I sit and when I rise,
you perceive my thoughts from afar. You discern my going out and my lying down; you
are familiar with all my ways* (Psalm 139:1–3).

_____

_____

_____

_____

_____

_____

_____

Truth #8: All People Have Significant Flaws and Defects

For all have sinned and fall short of the glory of God (Romans 3:23).

_____

_____

_____

_____

_____

_____

_____

Truth #9: People Cannot Earn Forgiveness, nor Should This Be Required of Them

Forgive one another if any of you has a grievance against someone (Colossians 3:13).

_____

_____

_____

_____

_____

_____

_____

_____

Look back through these truths about people. Which one do you have the easiest time believing? Which one do you have the hardest time believing? Why?

_____

_____

_____

_____

_____

_____

_____

_____

What specific person comes to mind when it comes to the truth you have the hardest time believing? How do you need to behave toward that person differently (for example, see the person as having worth, accept in spite of flaws, extend forgiveness even though the person isn't sorry for hurting you, stop pressuring the person to meet all your needs)?

_____

_____

_____

_____

_____

_____

_____

_____

Not only is it important to see yourself for who you really are, but you also need to see others for who they really are. If you don't see others accurately, you are going to treat them improperly. You must have the view of others that God has of you. Anything less will continue to lead the human race down the garden path of being abusive and denigrating toward one another, violating the second greatest commandment to love your neighbor as yourself.

Key Memory and Meditation Verses

Select three truths from the list in this lesson that speak the most powerfully to you. Spend some time this week meditating on the verses related to those truths so God can help you get the most meaning and significance from them as you can.

Contemplative Prayer
(to be read slowly, meditatively, and repeatedly)

Heavenly Father,

Help me to see other people the way You see them—fearfully and wonderfully made image-bearers who are precious to You. Help me to see others as fellow strugglers in the battle to resist their fallen nature who need my support and encouragement, just as I need theirs. Help me to take my needs to You and be appreciative when others allow You to work through them to meet the needs I have. Please empower me to accept people as they are while humbly engaging in iron-sharpening-iron relationships with others so we can help each other grow and mature.

Father, help me to value the uniqueness of people and know that each of us are your creative masterpieces and not meant to be carbon copies of one another. Empower me to enjoy the fact that others don't think, feel, or act exactly the way I do—and that this is a good thing because of how You can use it to form us into the image of your Son. Father, help me to forgive others when they hurt me and to humbly seek their forgiveness when I hurt them. Please, help me to love my neighbor and leave them better off by virtue of every interaction I have with them.

In the precious and holy name of Your Son, Jesus Christ, Amen.

THE LIES WE BELIEVE ABOUT LIFE

*The truth must essentially be regarded as in conflict with
this world; the world has never been so good and will never
become so good that the majority will desire the truth.*

SØREN KIERKEGAARD

The wisdom of this world is foolishness in God's sight.

1 CORINTHIANS 3:19

I'm a critic of new age psychobabble. Few things get me more lit up than the unbiblical platitudes that often come out of the pop-psyche world. When I see the latest version of what passes for wisdom in the secular landscape, I think of the statement the apostle Paul made when he wrote, "For the time will come when people will not put up with sound doctrine. Instead, to suit their own desires, they will gather around them a great number of teachers to say what their itching ears want to hear. They will turn their ears away from the truth and turn aside to myths" (2 Timothy 4:3–4). I believe we are living in those times, and in this lesson, we will explore five of what I consider to be the most destructive of these self-help teachings that are today passed around as "truth."

Assessing Your Beliefs

Complete the following self-assessment questionnaire on these teachings using the scale below. Note that as in previous lessons, I have added some additional lies not included in the accompanying *The Lies We Believe* book. I will tell you upfront that these are godless, unbiblical ways of thinking, but I want you to answer as honestly as you can as to whether or not you have adopted them into your view of life. In other words, be completely honest about the degree to which you believe these different views and try not to let the fact they are wrong influence your answer. As always, avoid using the neutral response (*4*) as much as possible.

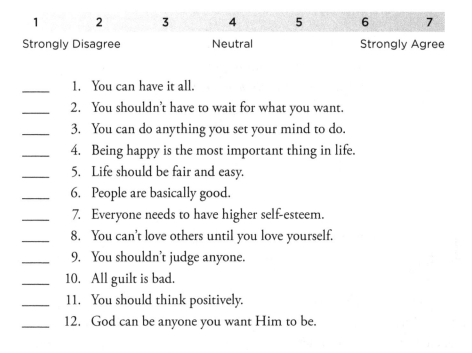

1	2	3	4	5	6	7
Strongly Disagree			Neutral			Strongly Agree

_____   1. You can have it all.

_____   2. You shouldn't have to wait for what you want.

_____   3. You can do anything you set your mind to do.

_____   4. Being happy is the most important thing in life.

_____   5. Life should be fair and easy.

_____   6. People are basically good.

_____   7. Everyone needs to have higher self-esteem.

_____   8. You can't love others until you love yourself.

_____   9. You shouldn't judge anyone.

_____ 10. All guilt is bad.

_____ 11. You should think positively.

_____ 12. God can be anyone you want Him to be.

From my perspective, these are all faulty ways of thinking about life. Unfortunately, these teachings tend to be offered to us as etched-in-stone truths from self-help books and seminars offered by "experts" in the field of personal growth and development. Look back through your answers and circle any statement you gave a *5* or higher, as these responses suggest you are looking at life in a destructive and unbiblical manner. I'm really not trying to rub your nose in it . . . just simply bringing it to your attention!

The Truth About These Lies

Let's turn our attention now to the truth. In the spaces provided below, write down why each of the following statements is unbiblical and likely to cause you problems in your life. You may not agree these are erroneous ways of thinking, and you may have a hard time coming up with a biblically solid rejoinder to these statements, so I've provided the biblical teaching for each statement. You will have to take it from there.

View #1: You Can Have It All

I denied myself nothing my eyes desired; I refused my heart no pleasure. . . . Yet when I surveyed all that my hands had done and what I toiled to achieve, everything was meaningless, a chasing after the wind; nothing was gained under the sun (Ecclesiastes 2:10–12).

_____

_____

_____

_____

_____

_____

View #2: You Shouldn't Have to Wait for What You Want

But they that wait upon the LORD shall renew their strength; they shall mount up with wings like eagles; they shall run, and not be weary; and they shall walk, and not faint (Isaiah 40:31 KJV).

The LORD is good to those who wait for Him, to the person who seeks Him (Lamentations 3:25 NASB).

_____

_____

_____

_____

_____

_____

View #3: You Can Do Anything You Set Your Mind to Do

Where were you when I laid the earth's foundation? Tell me, if you understand (Job 38:4).

_____

_____

_____

_____

_____

_____

View #4: Being Happy Is the Most Important Thing in Life

We who are strong ought to bear with the failings of the weak and not to please ourselves (Romans 15:1).

But the fruit of the Spirit is love, joy, peace, forbearance, kindness, goodness, faithfulness, gentleness, and self-control (Galatians 5:22–23).

_____

_____

_____

_____

_____

_____

View #5: Life Should Be Fair and Easy

There is something else meaningless that occurs on earth: the righteous who get what the wicked deserve, and the wicked who get what the righteous deserve (Ecclesiastes 8:14).

"I have told you these things, so that in me you may have peace. In this world you will have trouble" (John 16:33).

_____

_____

_____

_____

_____

_____

View #6: People Are Basically Good

There is no one righteous, not even one (Romans 3:10).

For I know that good itself does not dwell in me, that is, in my sinful nature (Romans 7:18).

_____

_____

_____

_____

_____

_____

_____

_____

_____

View #7: Everyone Needs to Have Higher Self-Esteem

Do not think of yourself more highly than you ought, but rather think of yourself with sober judgment, in accordance with the faith God has distributed to each of you (Romans 12:3).

Who, being in very nature God, did not consider equality with God something to be used to his own advantage; rather, he made himself nothing by taking the very nature of a servant, being made in human likeness. And being found in appearance as a man, he humbled himself by becoming obedient to death—even death on a cross (Philippians 2:6–8).

_____

_____

_____

_____

_____

_____

_____

_____

View #8: You Can't Love Others Until You Love Yourself

"But to you who are listening I say: Love your enemies, do good to those who hate you" (Luke 6:27).

"A new command I give you: Love one another. As I have loved you, so you must love one another" (John 13:34).

_____

_____

_____

_____

_____

_____

_____

_____

_____

_____

View #9: You Shouldn't Judge Anyone

Speak up and judge fairly; defend the rights of the poor and needy (Proverbs 31:9).

"You hypocrite, first take the plank out of your own eye, and then you will see clearly to remove the speck from your brother's eye" (Matthew 7:5).

Think of yourself with sober judgment (Romans 12:3).

_____

_____

_____

_____

_____

_____

_____

_____

_____

View #10: All Guilt Is Bad

Godly sorrow brings repentance that leads to salvation and leaves no regret, but worldly sorrow brings death (2 Corinthians 7:10).

For the worshipers would have been cleansed once for all, and would no longer have felt guilty for their sins (Hebrews 10:2).

_____

_____

_____

_____

_____

_____

_____

_____

_____

_____

View #11: You Should Think Positively

Brothers and sisters stop thinking like children (1 Corinthians 14:20).

Finally, brothers and sisters, whatever is true, whatever is noble, whatever is right, whatever is pure, whatever is lovely, whatever is admirable—if anything is excellent or praiseworthy—think about such things (Philippians 4:8).

_____

_____

_____

_____

_____

_____

_____

_____

_____

View #12: God Can Be Anyone You Want Him to Be

"To whom will you compare me? Or who is my equal?" says the Holy One (Isaiah 40:25).

For now we see only a reflection as in a mirror; then we shall see face to face
(1 Corinthians 13:12).

_____

_____

_____

_____

_____

_____

_____

_____

The bottom line is the world we live in is a frequent source of teachings and platitudes that are pleasant to hear but are simply not true. Adopting what "they" say may make us feel better, but is it *really* better for our souls?

- We want to hear that *we can have it all*—even though that is impossible, because choosing one thing always means not choosing something else.
- We want to believe *we shouldn't have to wait for what we want*, because that allows us to justify our impulsive and self-gratifying natures.
- We want to believe *we can do anything we set our mind to do*, because we don't want to face the fact that as finite and fallen human beings, there are limits to what we can do and what we can become in life.
- We want to think that *being happy is the most important thing in life*—even though we know becoming mature and God-honoring human beings is vastly more important.
- We want *life to be fair and easy*, though we know that it will be unfair and difficult at times.
- We want to believe that *people are basically good*, though we know there is nothing good or righteous about our fallen nature . . . and that turning that around requires supernatural power.

- We want to think *all any of us needs is more self-esteem*, when the truth is we need more humility about who we are.
- We want to accept the idea *we can't love others until we love ourselves*, because it gives us a hall pass on obeying the command to love other people no matter how we feel about ourselves.
- We want to buy into the false notion *we shouldn't ever judge other people's behavior*, when the Bible is clear that we just should not *arrogantly* judge other people as if we are better than them.
- We want to think that *all guilt is bad*, because true guilt over having done something wrong is painful and requires us to make amends.
- We want to believe *our thoughts should always be positive*, when in fact the Bible tells us to focus on what is true—whether it is positive or not.
- We want to believe *God can be anything we want Him to be*, because that allows us to justify seeing Him as our own Santa Claus who will give us whatever we want in this life.

I would argue the enemy wants you buy into what the world is teaching hook, line, and sinker so he can reel you into the boat of being discontented and anxious as you go through life. What "they" say is not the place to go in how to live your life. The Bible is the only valid source, and it provides the proper antidote for worldly teachings that "scratch your itching ears" but leave you worse off in the long run. So don't buy worldly wisdom. The apostle Paul was shooting straight with us when he wrote, "For the wisdom of this world is foolishness in God's sight" (1 Corinthians 3:19). When it comes to how to view life, let God work through His Word and "buy the truth and do not sell it" (Proverbs 23:23).

Key Memory and Meditation Verses

Select three lies from the list in this lesson that you tend to struggle with the most. Spend some time this week meditating on the verses that represent the biblical truths to counter each of those lies. Ask God to help you get the most meaning and significance from them as you can.

Contemplative Prayer
(to be read slowly, meditatively, and repeatedly)

Heavenly Father,

I pray that You will help me live in this world but not think the way the world does. Help me to accept that I can't have it all in life, to be patient in waiting for the things You want for me rather than impatiently going after all the things I want in the here-and-now, and to accept the limitations I have as a finite human being. Help me to know it isn't possible to achieve all the things I set my mind on, to not go out expecting life to be fair or easy, and to handle unfairness and difficulty the way Your Son did.

Father, I also ask that You would help me to see that all people have a fallen inclination to sin without thinking this makes people worthless or awful, to have an accurate sense of myself from the perspective of how I perform each day, neither thinking too highly of myself nor too lowly, and to actively love others regardless of how I feel about myself. Help me to refrain from being judgmental toward others while judging the actions of others the way You do, to see guilt about my sins is a healthy thing while not falling into self-hatred and self-condemnation, and to avoid the trap of "positive thinking" and instead focus my thoughts on what is true—whether they are positive or not. And help me to not turn You into who I want you to be but to see You as You truly are.

In the precious and holy name of Your Son, Jesus Christ, Amen.

THE LIES WE BELIEVE ABOUT GOD

The history of mankind will probably show that no
people has risen above its religion, and man's spiritual
history will positively demonstrate that no religion
has ever been greater than its idea of God.

A. W. TOZER

Religion that God our father accepts as pure and faultless
is this: to look after orphans and widows in their distress
and to keep oneself from being polluted by the world.

JAMES 1:27

Theologian A. W. Tozer was right when he said, "What comes into your mind when you think about God is the most important thing about you." Nothing is more important for determining how well or poorly you will go through life than your view of God. *Nothing.* Let me add another important truth to that statement: *How you view yourself is extremely important as well.* In fact, I would say what comes into your mind when you think about yourself is the second most important thing about you. Now, I am not suggesting that you adopt a narcissistic and self-centered attitude here, but simply that you recognize a well-lived life is tied to an accurate view of God as the Creator and have an accurate view of yourself as His creature.

Assessing Your Beliefs

Even though you already assessed some faulty beliefs about God in lesson one, I want you to do it again using the following self-assessment inventory. You will notice that I have included some additional faulty views of God for you to consider. Even though you know these are all inaccurate views of God, be as honest as you can about whether or not you view God in these ways. As always, avoid using the neutral response (4) as much as possible.

1	2	3	4	5	6	7
Strongly Disagree			Neutral			Strongly Agree

_____   1. God's love must be earned.

_____   2. God is mean and vindictive.

_____   3. God ignores our disobedience.

_____   4. God wants you to have it all.

_____   5. God has lost control of everything.

_____   6. God is supposed to give me everything I want in life.

_____   7. God is more interested in rules than relationships.

_____   8. God has abandoned me.

_____   9. God has no empathy or compassion about what I'm going through.

_____   10. God is disgusted with me.

_____   11. God has rejected me.

_____   12. God can be anyone you want him to be.

Look back through your answers and circle any statement you gave a *5* or higher, as these responses indicate you agree with a false view of God. In this lesson we will focus on the critical task of addressing these faulty views you have about God, as the enemy will use any lies you believe about Him to torpedo your time on earth.

How You View God

Every single human being on the planet has distorted views of God—ways of thinking about Him that fall short of just how amazing and awesome He truly is. In Psalm 47:2, we read, "For the LORD Most High is awesome, the great King over all the earth." If we look honestly at how we view God, we don't come anywhere close to seeing Him that way. Truth be told, we tend to see God in a way that is far below His dignity and perfection. With this in mind, review each of the attributes about God listed below, read the corresponding verse, and then write down in your own words what this attribute means to you in terms of how you view God.

Attribute #1: God Is Self-Existent

How great is God—beyond our understanding! The number of his years is past finding out (Job 36:26).

Before the mountains were born or you brought forth the whole world, from everlasting to everlasting you are God (Psalm 90:2).

_____

_____

_____

_____

_____

Attribute #2: God Is All-Powerful

I know that you can do all things; no purpose of yours can be thwarted (Job 42:2).

"With man this is impossible, but with God all things are possible" (Matthew 19:26).

_____

_____

_____

_____

_____

Attribute #3: God Is Everywhere-at-Once

The heavens, even the highest heaven, cannot contain you (1 Kings 8:27).

Where can I go from your spirit? Where can I flee from your presence? If I go up to the heavens, you are there; if I make my bed in the depths, you are there (Psalm 139:7–8).

_____

_____

_____

_____

_____

_____

Attribute #4: God Is All-Knowing

Great is our Lord and mighty in power; his understanding has no limit (Psalm 147:5).

Oh, the depth of the riches of the wisdom and knowledge of God! How unsearchable his judgments, and his paths beyond tracing out! (Romans 11:33).

_____

_____

_____

_____

_____

Attribute #5: God Is Holy

Who is like you—majestic in holiness, awesome in glory, working wonders? (Exodus 15:11).

Holy, holy, holy is the LORD almighty (Isaiah 6:3).

_____

_____

_____

_____

_____

Attribute #6: God Is Good

Good and upright is the LORD *(Psalm 25:8).*

The LORD *is good to all; he has compassion on all he has made (Psalm 145:9).*

_____

_____

_____

_____

_____

_____

Attribute #7: God Is Just

A faithful God who does no wrong, upright and just is he (Deuteronomy 32:4).

Great and marvelous are your deeds, Lord God Almighty. Just and true are your ways, King of the nations (Revelation 15:3).

_____

_____

_____

_____

_____

_____

Attribute #8: God Is Merciful

"Be merciful, just as your Father is merciful" (Luke 6:36).

I will have mercy on whom I have mercy, and I will have compassion on whom I have compassion (Romans 9:15).

_____

_____

_____

_____

_____

_____

Attribute #9: God Is Sovereign

Dominion belongs to the LORD and he rules over the nations (Psalm 22:28).

The LORD does whatever pleases him, in the heavens and on the earth, in the seas and all their depths (Psalm 135:6).

_____

_____

_____

_____

_____

_____

Attribute #10: God Is Unchanging

I the LORD do not change (Malachi 3:6).

Jesus Christ is the same yesterday and today and forever (Hebrews 13:8).

_____

_____

_____

_____

_____

_____

Attribute #11: God Is Love

"For God so loved the world that he gave his one and only Son" (John 3:16).

God is love (1 John 4:8).

_____

_____

_____

_____

_____

_____

Keep asking God to help you believe these things about Him in the deepest part of your being. God wants you to see Him for who He really is—and you are not going to have the close and loving relationship He wants to have with you if you have a distorted view of Him. The more deeply and accurately you see God for who He truly is, the deeper your relationship with Him will be and the less you will worry about or get caught up in the snares of life.

Key Memory and Meditation Verses

Select three attributes of God from the list in this lesson that speak the most powerfully to you. Spend some time this week meditating on the verses related to those truths so God can help you get the most meaning and significance from them as you can.

Contemplative Prayer
(to be read slowly, meditatively, and repeatedly)

Heavenly Father,

You are the one and only God, with no equal in the universe. Please help me to see You for who You truly are. Thank You that You are love and that Your love for me has no dimensions or limitations. Thank You for being neither shaming nor condemning toward me concerning the wrong things I have done, but for bathing them in grace and forgiveness. Thank You for being sovereignly in control of all things that are happening here on earth and for Your promise that you will bring things to a just close one day.

Father, I thank You also for having goodwill toward me, that You are out to help me and not harm me, that You love me enough to discipline me when I step out of line, that You are extravagant in the gifts you have given me, that in You there is no falsehood but only truth, that You graciously co-labor with me to help me grow and mature, and that You are not going to let anything stand in Your way of redeeming a fallen world. Father, please help me to break free from the distorted ways I see You and to grow in seeing You as the great and awesome God You are.

In the precious and holy name of Your Son, Jesus Christ, Amen.

THE LIES MEN BELIEVE

*Waste no more time arguing what a
good man should be. Be one.*

MARCUS AURELIUS

*When I became a man, I put the
ways of childhood behind me.*

1 CORINTHIANS 13:11

In *The Lies We Believe*, I suggested there are faulty ways of thinking that are fairly unique to the male persuasion. The point of the chapter wasn't to imply that *all* men think in these unbiblical ways or that women don't have their own version of these misbeliefs. However, I do believe the majority of men fall into believing the five lies we explored in that chapter. In this lesson, I want men to drill down further into these lies and allow God to help them move in the direction of a more accurate view of themselves as men.

Now, this may seem strange to ask, but I would like female readers to complete this lesson as well. Specifically, I want you to ask yourself if you view men from any of these unbiblical perspectives and if you possibly might be colluding with or enabling the men in your life to keep thinking in these unbiblical ways. When we get to the next lesson on the truth about women, I will ask the men to do the same—to ask themselves if they are seeing females through the same faulty lenses that some women see themselves.

Assessing Your Beliefs

Before we get to work on overcoming the lies we believe about men, I want you to complete the following self-assessment inventory. Note that I have added some new faulty beliefs for you to consider in each of the areas of the lies we are going to explore. Even though you know every statement listed below about men is false, be as honest as you can about the degree to which you agree with the statement. Avoid using the neutral response (4) as much as possible.

1	2	3	4	5	6	7
Strongly Disagree			Neutral			Strongly Agree

_____ 1. I don't have what it takes to be a man.

_____ 2. It's not okay to feel sad, scared, or hurt.

_____ 3. My good intentions ought to satisfy everyone.

_____ 4. Sex is about my pleasure and enjoyment.

_____ 5. I can do everything on my own.

_____ 6. I don't need other men in my life to support or encourage me.

_____ 7. My hidden sins are not harming me or others.

_____ 8. I'm in control of my future.

_____ 9. More entertainment/pleasure will make my life happier and more meaningful.

_____ 10. My anger isn't a problem in my relationships with others.

_____ 11. I'm not responsible for how I react to people who mistreat me.

_____ 12. It's okay to enable other men's unrighteousness.

_____ 13. I see all my flaws and defects.

_____ 14. A real man grabs for all the gusto he can in life.

_____ 15. I don't need to mature any further because I'm fine as I am.

Look back through your answers and circle any statement you gave a *5* or higher, as these responses would suggest you are looking at yourself (or the man in your life) in a destructive and unbiblical manner. Next, we will turn our attention to arguing against these unbiblical views of manhood.

The Truth About These Lies

In the spaces provided below, write down why each of the following statements are unbiblical and likely to cause you problems in your life. You may not agree these are erroneous ways of thinking, but nevertheless, I want you to think about what the truth is and move in that direction. God is more than happy to guide you to the truth on these unbiblical ways of thinking.

View #1: I Don't Have What It Takes to Be a Man

_____

_____

_____

_____

_____

_____

_____

View #2: It's Not Okay to Feel Sad, Scared, or Hurt

_____

_____

_____

_____

_____

_____

_____

View #3: My Good Intentions Ought to Satisfy Everyone

_____

_____

_____

_____

_____

_____

_____

View #4: Sex Is About My Pleasure and Enjoyment

_____

_____

_____

_____

_____

_____

View #5: I Can Do Everything on My Own

_____

_____

_____

_____

_____

_____

View #6: I Don't Need Other Men in My Life to Support and Encourage Me

_____

_____

_____

_____

_____

_____

View #7: My Hidden Sins Are Not Harming Me or Others

_____

_____

_____

_____

_____

_____

View #8: I'm In Control of My Own Future

_____
_____
_____
_____
_____

**View #9: More Entertainment/Pleasure Will Make
My Life Happier and More Meaningful**

_____
_____
_____
_____
_____

View #10: My Anger Isn't a Problem in My Relationships with Others

_____
_____
_____
_____
_____

**View #11: I'm Not Responsible for How I
React to People Who Mistreat Me**

_____
_____
_____
_____
_____
_____

View #12: It's Okay to Enable Other Men's Unrighteousness

_____

_____

_____

_____

_____

_____

View #13: I See All My Flaws and Defects

_____

_____

_____

_____

_____

_____

View #14: A Real Man Grabs for All the Gusto He Can in Life

_____

_____

_____

_____

_____

_____

_____

View #15: I Don't Need to Mature Any Further Because I'm Fine as I Am

_____

_____

_____

_____

_____

_____

_____

The truth will set us free, but it often stings at first. This is certainly true when it comes to looking at these lies that men tend to believe about themselves. The reality is that we must square up with the fact we have a lot of unbiblical ways of thinking about authentic manhood that we need God's help to overcome and replace with the truth:

- As men, we do have "what it takes to me a man," because we have the Holy Spirit inside of us.
- It is okay for us to feel sad, scared, and hurt, because those are healthy and appropriate emotions to feel given what life throws our way.
- Our good intentions are not enough—we always need to back them up with action.
- Sex is about the mutual pleasure and satisfaction of both marital partners
- We can't successfully go through life doing everything on our own—we need the help of others.
- We need other men in our lives to support and encourage us, especially given how often we get discouraged and want to throw in the towel.
- The sins we hide from others are damaging not only to ourselves but also to the people we love, because sin harms our ability to healthily bond with others.
- We are not in control of our future and need to put our faith and trust in God for how things turn out.
- More levels of entertainment and pleasure do not translate into a happier and more meaningful life . . . only a life that is more hedonistic.
- Our anger, whether we stuff it or spew it, is a serious problem in our relationships with others.
- We are fully responsible for how we respond to people who mistreat us.
- It is wrong to collude with other men to enable them to act out their unrighteous and evil ways of going through life (think Hitler).
- All of us are blind to some degree to the many flaws and defects we have— and we need to be aware of that fact.
- A real man healthily grabs for all the relational gusto he can have in life with family and friends.
- We all have a lot more maturing to do—we will never fully attain the maturity of Christ during our lifetime.

Don't grow weary. The enemy wants to "kill and steal and destroy" your manhood, and these lies are a major part of his strategy for accomplishing that agenda in your life. So don't give in to his "fiery darts" and believe any of these lies about yourself. Spend the rest of your life moving forward with *God's* truth about who you really are as a man.

Key Memory and Meditation Verses

So be strong, act like a man, and observe what the Lord your God requires: Walk in obedience to him, and keep his decrees and commands, his laws and regulations, as written in the Law of Moses (1 Kings 2:2–3).

Blessed is the one who does not walk in step with the wicked or stand in the way that sinners take or sit in the company of mockers, but whose delight is in the law of the Lord, and who meditates on his law day and night (Psalm 1:1–2).

When I was a child, I talked like a child, I thought like a child, I reasoned like a child. When I became a man, I put the ways of childhood behind me (1 Corinthians 13:11).

Husbands, love your wives, just as Christ love the church and gave himself up for her (Ephesians 5:25).

Fathers, do not exasperate your children; instead, bring them up in the training and instruction of the Lord (Ephesians 6:4).

But you, man of God, flee from all this, and pursue righteousness, godliness, faith, love, endurance and gentleness (1 Timothy 6:11).

Contemplative Prayer
(to be read slowly, meditatively, and repeatedly)

Heavenly Father,

Thank You for equipping me with everything I need to be a godly man. Help me to experience painful emotions rather than run from them, act on my good intentions, focus on the sexual pleasure of my spouse, include others in my life rather than try to go it alone, and turn to other men for support and encouragement. Help me to have empathy about how my sins are hurtful to others, accept that I'm not in control, and turn to you rather than pleasurable entertainment for a greater sense of meaning and purpose.

Father, I also ask that You help me to face the fact that my anger is a problem that I need to address. Help me to take responsibility for how I respond to those who wound me, refuse to enable the evil actions of other men, and refuse to live in denial about my flaws and defects. Show me how I can reach out and grasp the abundant life You provide rather than earthly gusto and embrace the journey of authentic manhood by growing and maturing in my life. Thank You for showing me what a real man looks life in the life of Jesus Christ—and help me to become more like Him.

In the precious and holy name of Your Son, Jesus Christ, Amen.

THE LIES WOMEN BELIEVE

I want to do it because I want to do it. Women must
try to do things as men have tried. When they fail,
their failure must be but a challenge to others.

AMELIA EARHART

She is clothed with strength and dignity; she can
laugh at the days to come. She speaks with wisdom,
and faithful instruction is on her tongue.

PROVERBS 31:25–26

It's a bit risky to suggest there are certain lies that men and women are uniquely prone to believe, because this could be interpreted as an effort to stereotype and even denigrate the sexes. This is certainly not my intent. So, as we turn our attention to the lies women believe, I want you to know I have bent over backward to select lies that are not the least bit intended to paint women into a stereotypical or dismissive corner as to how they falsely view themselves. My hope is to simply heighten men and women's awareness of the enemy's evil efforts to "kill and steal and destroy" with the specific lies he wants each gender to believe. He has uniquely designed these lies to try to keep all of us from experiencing the abundant life Christ has for us.

Assessing Your Beliefs

As I focused the previous lesson on the lies men believe about themselves, I want to invite women to take the following self-assessment to evaluate whether they are thinking about one another in these unbiblical ways. Note that once again, I have added some additional lies that women might believe about themselves. Even though you know every statement listed about women is false, be as honest as you can about the degree to which you agree with each statement. As always, avoid using the neutral response (*4*) as much as possible. Here we go.

1	2	3	4	5	6	7
Strongly Disagree			Neutral			Strongly Agree

_____ 1. My main job in life is to make everyone happy.

_____ 2. It's not okay to speak my mind.

_____ 3. I'm honestly facing my flaws and defects.

_____ 4. I'm not worthy of being loved for who I am.

_____ 5. Outer beauty is more important than inner beauty.

_____ 6. I'm worthless and don't have much to offer.

_____ 7. The sinful things I do are relatively harmless.

_____ 8. I'm entitled to love and respect.

_____ 9. The wrong things I've done are beyond God's forgiveness.

_____ 10. My feelings are the best guide to what is true.

_____ 11. My worth and identity are tied to whether or not I have a man in my life.

_____ 12. How my children turn out is a reflection of me.

_____ 13. I'm not as messed up as other women I know.

_____ 14. Women are less capable and competent than men.

_____ 15. It's okay to tolerate and even enable misogyny.

Look back through your answers and circle any statement you gave a *5* or higher, as these responses would suggest that you are looking at yourself (or the woman in your life) in a destructive and unbiblical manner. Next, we will turn our attention to arguing against these unbiblical views of womanhood.

The Truth About These Lies

In the spaces provided below, write down why each of the following views are unbiblical and likely to cause you problems in your life. You may not agree these are erroneous ways of thinking, but nevertheless, I want you to think about the truth related to each lie and move in that direction. God is more than happy to guide you to the truth on these unbiblical ways of thinking.

View #1: My Main Job in Life Is to Make Everyone Happy

_____

_____

_____

_____

_____

_____

_____

View #2: It's Not Okay to Speak My Mind

_____

_____

_____

_____

_____

_____

_____

View #3: I'm Honestly Facing My Flaws and Defects

_____

_____

_____

_____

_____

_____

_____

View #4: I'm Not Worthy of Being Loved for Who I Am

_____

_____

_____

_____

_____

_____

View #5: Outer Beauty Is More Important Than Inner Beauty

_____

_____

_____

_____

_____

_____

_____

View #6: I'm Worthless and Don't Have Much to Offer

_____

_____

_____

_____

_____

_____

View #7: The Sinful Things I Do Are Relatively Harmless

_____

_____

_____

_____

_____

_____

View #8: I'm Entitled to Love and Respect

_____
_____
_____
_____
_____
_____

View #9: The Wrong Things I've Done Are Beyond God's Forgiveness

_____
_____
_____
_____
_____
_____

View #10: My Feelings Are the Best Guide to What Is True

_____
_____
_____
_____
_____
_____

View #11: My Worth and Identity Are Tied to Whether or Not I Have a Man in My Life

_____
_____
_____
_____
_____
_____

View #12: How My Children Turn Out Is a Reflection of Me

_____

_____

_____

_____

_____

_____

View #13: I'm Not As Messed Up As Other Women I Know

_____

_____

_____

_____

_____

_____

_____

_____

View #14: Women Are Less Capable and Competent Than Men

_____

_____

_____

_____

_____

_____

_____

View #15: It's Okay to Tolerate and Even Enable Misogyny

_____

_____

_____

_____

_____

_____

Ladies, forgive me for having the audacity to say this, but you must face the fact you have as many unbiblical ways of thinking about authentic womanhood as men do about authentic manhood. You need God's help to renew your mind just as much as men do so you can replace these unbiblical ways of thinking with the truth:

- Your main job in life isn't to make everyone happy—it is to love God with all your heart, mind, soul, and strength, and to love your neighbor as yourself.
- All of us struggle with some degree of denial about the things that are wrong with us—we need to be aware of that fact and not run from it.
- You are worthy of being loved for who you are, warts and all, because God made you in His image—and you are not to be mistreated.
- Inner beauty is a thousand times more important than outer beauty, whether the world we live in sees it that way or not.
- The sinful things you do—even the "small" ones—are not harmless and are causing you and others more damage and harm than you know.
- You are not entitled to love and respect, but it is certainly appropriate for you to desire both from the people in your life.
- Nothing you can ever do is beyond the forgiveness of God—*nothing*.
- While you should not deny what you feel, feelings are not the best guide to what is true—only what God says is the best guide to truth.
- How you raise your children is a reflection of you, but how your children turn out is a reflection of their own choices that they make in life.
- You are as messed up as the other women you know—even the deeply troubled women you know—because compared to Christ, we all fall far short of His glory and perfection.
- While a particular man or woman might be more competent and capable than you at certain things, neither men nor women are inherently more competent and capable than the other simply because of their gender.
- It's never okay to tolerate, much less enable, misogyny in other people, whether they be male or female.

Don't grow weary. The enemy wants to "kill and steal and destroy" your womanhood, and these lies are a major part of his strategy for accomplishing this agenda in your life. So, don't give in to his "fiery darts" and believe any of these lies about yourself. Spend the rest of your life internalizing God's truth about who you are as a woman.

Key Memory and Meditation Verses

I praise you because I am fearfully and wonderfully made; your works are wonderful, I know that full well (Psalm 139:14).

She is clothed with strength and dignity; she can laugh at the days to come. She speaks with wisdom, and faithful instruction is on her tongue (Proverbs 31:25–26).

Charm is deceptive, and beauty is fleeting; but a woman who fears the LORD is to be praised. Honor her for all her hands have done, and let her works bring her praise at the city gate (Proverbs 31:30–31).

In the same way, the women are to be worthy of respect, not malicious talkers but temperate and trustworthy in everything (1 Timothy 3:11).

For the Spirit God gave us does not make us timid, but gives us power, love and self-discipline (2 Timothy 1:7).

Your beauty should not come from outward adornment, such as elaborate hairstyles and the wearing of gold jewelry or fine clothes. Rather, it should be that of your inner self, the unfading beauty of a gentle and quiet spirit, which is of great worth in God's sight (1 Peter 3:3–4).

Contemplative Prayer
(to be read slowly, meditatively, and repeatedly)

Heavenly Father,

Thank You for making me in Your image and unconditionally loving me as Your precious daughter. Help me to see that my job in life is to love You and my neighbor with all my strength, to have my own confident voice in speaking to others as I encounter difficult situations, and to face my own defects rather than focus on the flaws in others. Help me to understand I am worthy of love as I am, to work on growing in inner beauty, and to believe that because of how You made me, I have great things to offer to others.

Father, I also ask You to help me to develop greater empathy about how my sins hurt others, accept that I am not entitled to love but wired to desire it, grasp that none of my sins are beyond Your forgiveness, and acknowledge my feelings but base my actions on the truth. Help me to put my worth and identity in being made in Your image, accept that how my children turn out will be a reflection of the choices they make, humbly admit I am as flawed as anyone else, embrace that You have equipped me to be as competent and capable as men, and never support the mistreatment of women—whether it is by men or other women. Thank You, Father, for making me the person that I am. I pray that You will help me to stay the course in growing into healthier and more authentic womanhood as my life plays out.

In the precious and holy name of Your Son, Jesus Christ, Amen.

PART THREE

THE TRUTHS
WE MUST
BELIEVE

THE TRUTH ABOUT
THE TRUTH

*Seek the truth, listen to the truth, teach the truth, love
the truth, abide by the truth, and defend the truth.*

JOHN HUS

*Buy the truth and do not sell it—wisdom,
instruction and insight as well.*

PROVERBS 23:23

Before we begin this lesson, I want to remind you that the truth has certain qualities you need to keep in mind as you work on the process of renewing your mind. If you don't fully embrace these truths about the truth, you are not going to make as much progress in renewing your mind as is available to you—and this will "lower the ceiling" on the degree of spiritual, emotional, and relational health that is possible in your life. So, with this in mind, let's begin by looking at some of the important characteristics of truth. As I go through each one, I want you to write down your honest thoughts about the degree to which you see truth that way.

Truth Comes Piece by Piece

American novelist Anais Nin once said that truth is like an elaborate puzzle that can only be put together "fragment by fragment, on a small scale, by successive developments, cellularly, like a laborious mosaic."[2] We cannot afford to approach it any other way—we have to humble ourselves in acquiring truth and be patient about the fact it is a lifelong process that we will never complete. How do you see truth along these lines?

_____

_____

_____

_____

_____

_____

_____

Truth Is Not Ours

Truth is not our possession—it belongs to God. The Bible says, "Guide me in *your* truth," not "Guide me in what *we* think the truth is" (Psalm 25:5). There is no truth we will ever discover that God didn't already know and possess. Every truth belongs to God. If we don't see things the way He does, we're the ones who are wrong. And when we stumble across an important truth, we need to humbly acknowledge we found something that was God's all along and He was gracious enough to let us find it. In light of this, there isn't any such thing as "your truth" or "my truth," only God's truth. How do you see truth along these lines?

_____

_____

_____

_____

_____

_____

_____

Truth Is a Prerequisite for Personal Growth

The truth, not lies, sets people free to grow into healthy human beings. This is why all of us need to dedicate ourselves to the pursuit of truth—it is the only way to mature into the loving people God wants us to be. Just as healthy food is necessary for healthy physical growth, and unhealthy food will damage the physical body, the same is true of truth. Truth is healthy nutrition for the mind. Remember, it's "garbage in, garbage out" when it comes to the thoughts we have each day. How do you see truth along these lines?

_____

_____

_____

_____

_____

_____

_____

Truth Has Barriers

Our "thinkers" have been broken since the fall of humankind. For this reason, there are numerous barriers we will encounter to the truth, including (1) *ignorance*, (2) *incomplete knowledge*, (3) *distractedness*, (4) *intellectual pride*, (5) *forgetfulness*, (6) *intellectual laziness and apathy*, (6) *drawing wrong conclusions*, (7) *closed-mindedness and dogmatism*, (8) *intellectual fatigue*, (9) *inconsistencies*, and (10) *faulty perspectives*. Which of these do you tend to fall into that are costing you a more accurate sense of how things really are in life?

_____

_____

_____

_____

_____

_____

Truth Often Leads to Pain

You have probably heard the statement, "The truth will set you free, but first it will make you miserable." Like it or not, there are a lot of truths that trigger spiritual and emotional pain. There are times when biblical truth will punch us in the stomach and make us feel humbled, convicted, and even rebuked. What are some of the more painful biblical truths you have had to face as a follower of Christ?

_____
_____
_____
_____
_____
_____
_____
_____

Truth Requires Doubt

We all need to be a "doubting" Thomas as we go through life (see John 20:25). The genuine pursuit of truth requires doubt. Philosopher Rene Descartes said, "If you would be a real seeker after truth, it is necessary that at least once in your life you doubt, as far as possible, all things." What are some of the truths you have doubted that led you to greater assurance they were true? What truths do you need to doubt for God to embed them more firmly in your life?

_____
_____
_____
_____
_____
_____
_____
_____

Truth Will Stand Forever

The prophet Isaiah wrote, "The grass withers and the flowers fall, but the word of our God endures forever" (40:8). In a day and age when people say there are "alternative facts" and "the truth isn't the truth," do you believe the truth as identified by God is unchanging and will last forever? Do you believe the Bible is shooting straight when it says, "God is not human, that he should lie, not a human being, that he should change his mind" (Numbers 23:19)?

_____

_____

_____

_____

_____

Adjust to the Truth

As you go through life, it is important to understand the truth has certain qualities and characteristics you have to accept and to which you need to adjust. The analogy I use with clients is that if you were to take up the sport of tennis, you would have to comply with the requirements of what it takes to get the ball successfully over the net. For example, you could decide to hit the ball with the handle of your racquet rather than the strings, but you would never be very good at tennis—you have to hit the ball with the strings if you want to play well. Similarly, to renew your mind successfully, you have to adjust to the fact that God is truth, He has wired the truth with certain properties and requirements, and He isn't going to adjust the truth in our efforts to grow psychologically, relationally, and spiritually. When it comes to the truth, we adjust to it . . . or we play life poorly.

Key Memory and Meditation Verses

Guide me in your truth and teach me, for you are God my Savior, and my hope is in you all day long (Psalm 25:5).

The grass withers and the flowers fall, but the word of our God endures forever (Isaiah 40:8).

For the law was given through Moses; grace and truth came through Jesus Christ (John 1:17).

But when he, the Spirit of truth, comes, he will guide you into all truth (John 16:13).

But for those . . . who reject the truth and follow evil, there will be wrath and anger (Romans 2:8).

For we cannot do anything against the truth, but only for the truth (2 Corinthians 13:8).

Contemplative Prayer
(to be read slowly, meditatively, and repeatedly)

Heavenly Father,

You are truth, and in You there is no hint of falsehood or deception. I know that what You say is true and that I can base my life on it. Help me to respect the fact that truth is acquired piece by piece, that truth is your possession and not mine, and to embrace that truth is the path to growth. Please remove any barriers in my mind and heart that keep me from seeing the truth accurately; accept that truth is often painful; be willing to doubt what I believe so You can show me the truth and erase my doubts; and embrace that truth will stand forever because you will stand forever.

Father, I pray that You will also help me to exercise humility when turning to You to guide me to truth, knowing that my finite mind will never grasp but the smallest piece of what You know and understand completely. In a world where truth is under fire and seems to change from moment to moment, I thank You that Your truth never changes, because You never change. Please, Father, help me to find the courage to face the truth and apply it to my life on a daily basis.

In the precious and holy name of Your Son, Jesus Christ. Amen.

TO ERR IS HUMAN

If at first you don't succeed, you're running about average.

M. H. ALDERSON

All have sinned and fall short of the glory of God.

ROMANS 3:23

More than a few of us beat ourselves up for making mistakes as we go through life. The fact we do this in spite of knowing we are error-prone humans suggests we have an unconscious desire to be God—a perfect, flawless, never-make-a-mistake being. The mistakes we make each day are a painful reminder we fall short of God's perfection, but rather than accept this and extend grace to ourselves, we tend to condemn and denigrate ourselves. During this lesson, I want to challenge you to work on moving away from expecting yourself to be perfect while moving in the direction of striving to be excellent.

Wanting to Be God's Equal

There are three ways we unconsciously desire to be God's equal. First, we want to be all-knowing so we never make mistakes. Second, we want to be all-powerful so everything will be under our control. Third, we want to be everywhere-at-once so we can get three million things done a day and never have anything left over to do tomorrow. In the space provided below, write down examples of where you have beat yourself up in each of these areas: for making a mistake, for getting upset when something was out of your control, and for becoming frustrated when you didn't get as much done as you had hoped.

Situations Where I Beat Myself Up for Making Mistakes

_____

_____

_____

_____

_____

_____

Situations Where I Got Upset About Things I Couldn't Control

_____

_____

_____

_____

_____

_____

_____

Situations Where I Became Frustrated About Not Getting Enough Done

_____

_____

_____

_____

_____

_____

Adjusting Your Mindset

Review each of the situations you just wrote down. Next, write down the *correct* thoughts you need to have about each situation to handle it properly in your mind.

The Right Thoughts About Making Mistakes

_____
_____
_____
_____
_____
_____
_____

The Right Thoughts About Not Being Able to Control Situations

_____
_____
_____
_____
_____
_____
_____
_____

The Right Thoughts About Not Getting Everything Done

_____
_____
_____
_____
_____
_____
_____
_____

I encourage you to keep moving away from critical and condemning thoughts (lies) in each of these areas and moving toward compassionate and humble thoughts (truth). The enemy wants you to keep trying to be God's equal—to continually pursue being all-knowing, all-powerful, and everywhere-at-once. He knows that if he can do this, you will continue to shame and denigrate yourself for being a finite, fallen human being who—even on your best day—can't come within a million miles of being God.

Perfectionism or Excellence?

God wants us to filter life through a mindset of *excellence*. He wants us to be *realistic* and *process-minded* and to gain our *worth from being fearfully and wonderfully made in His image*. Although He knows we will be *discouraged at times*, we are to *keep trying*, to *welcome feedback and correction*, to *correct our mistakes*, and to *keep moving forward*. This means we need to let go of our *perfectionistic* mindset—that *idealistic* and *product-minded* attitude that tells us we get our *worth from performance*, gets easily *overwhelmed* to the point of *giving up*, *resists feedback*, and *remembers mistakes*.

Making Mistakes

A mindset of *excellence* will set us free. A mindset of *perfectionism* will do us in. With this in mind, consider three mistakes you've made recently. In the space below, write down what your perfectionistic thoughts were versus what you would have thought had you filtered the mistake through a mindset of excellence.

Event #1: _____

Perfectionistic Mindset:

_____

_____

_____

Excellence Mindset:

_____

_____

_____

Event #2: _____

Perfectionistic Mindset:

_____

_____

_____

Excellence Mindset:

_____

_____

_____

Event #3: _____

Perfectionistic Mindset:

_____

_____

_____

Excellence Mindset:

_____

_____

_____

Loss of Control

Now consider three situations where you didn't have control over things. In the space below, write down what your perfectionistic thoughts were versus what you would have thought had you filtered not having control through the mindset of excellence.

Event #1: _____

Perfectionistic Mindset:

_____

_____

_____

Excellence Mindset:

_____

_____

_____

Event #2: _____

Perfectionistic Mindset:

_____

_____

_____

Excellence Mindset:

_____

_____

_____

Event #3: _____

Perfectionistic Mindset:

_____

_____

_____

Excellence Mindset:

_____

_____

_____

Not Getting Everything Done

Finally, consider three situations where you didn't get as much done as you would have liked. In the space provided on the next page, write down what your perfectionistic thoughts were versus what you would have thought had you filtered not everything getting done through the mindset of excellence.

Event #1: _____

Perfectionistic Mindset:

_____

_____

_____

Excellence Mindset:

_____

_____

_____

Event #2: _____

Perfectionistic Mindset:

_____

_____

_____

Excellence Mindset:

_____

_____

_____

Event #3: _____

Perfectionistic Mindset:

_____

_____

_____

Excellence Mindset:

_____

_____

_____

Keep working on taking your perfectionistic thoughts captive (I shouldn't have lost my car keys . . . no one else does such stupid things . . . I'm never going to get my act together) and replacing them with thoughts of excellence (it's okay to misplace my car keys . . . I'm only human . . . it doesn't mean I'm stupid). Consider rereading the accompanying chapter "To Err Is Human" in *The Lies We Believe* to let these truths settle more deeply in your soul.

Don't forget to keep doing your *TRUTH Journal* every day. It is important for you to track all five parts of the model—(1) the unhealthy emotions and behaviors you have, (2) the external events that trigger you, (3) the ruined (faulty) thoughts through which you filter the events, (4) the right thoughts you needed to filter the events through, and (5) the impact having the right thoughts had on your emotions and actions.

Key Memory and Meditation Verses

To all perfection I see a limit, but your commands are boundless (Psalm 119:96).

This righteousness is given through faith in Jesus Christ to all who believe. There is no difference between Jew and Gentile, for all have sinned and fall short of the glory of God (Romans 3:22–23).

I do not understand what I do. For what I want to do I do not do, but what I hate I do. . . . I know that good itself does not dwell in me, that is, in my sinful nature. For I have the desire to do what is good but cannot carry it out (Romans 7:15, 18).

The acts of the flesh are obvious: sexual immorality, impurity and debauchery; idolatry and witchcraft; hatred, discord, jealousy, fits of rage, selfish ambition, dissentions, factions and envy; drunkenness, orgies, and the like (Galatians 5:19–21).

As for you, you were dead in your transgressions and sins. . . . All of us lived among them at one time, gratifying the cravings of the flesh and following its desires and thoughts. Like the rest, we were by nature deserving of wrath (Ephesians 2:1, 3).

If perfection could have been attained through the Levitical priesthood . . . why was there still a need for another priest to come, one in the order of Melchizedek, not in the order of Aaron? (Hebrews 7:11).

Contemplative Prayer
(to be read slowly, meditatively, and repeatedly)

Heavenly Father,

I pray for Your help to accept my fallenness without indulging in it. Please help me to humbly accept that, unlike you, I have only limited knowledge while I'm here on earth, have little power over the things that happen to me, and can only accomplish so much each day. You are all-knowing, all-powerful, and everywhere-at-once—there are no limits to what You know, what You can do, or the amount You can get done moment by moment.

Please help me, Father, to stop comparing myself to You or trying to be Your equal. Allow me to accept that I am a human being and prone to making mistakes because I am not You. Again, I ask that You help me to accept that fact without indulging my fallenness so Your grace might abound. Help me to stop pursuing perfection and to instead pursue excellence—thinking realistically rather than idealistically, being process-minded rather than product-minded, striving to be my best rather than the best, and tying my worth to being your image-bearer rather than how well or poorly I do things.

Father, help me press on to the mark of being more like Your Son over time and not shame or condemn myself that I'm not already like Him. Please, Father, help me to be open to corrective feedback, even when it is unlovingly spoken, and put myself in Your hands for polishing off all the rough edges of who I am.

In the precious and holy name of Your Son, Jesus Christ. Amen.

You Can't Please Everyone

I cannot give you the formula for success, but I can give
you the formula for failure—try to please everybody.

HERBERT BAYARD SWOPE

Am I now trying to win the approval of human beings, or of
God? Or am I trying to please people? If I were still trying
to please people, I would not be a servant of Christ.

GALATIANS 1:10

We all have an unhealthy people pleaser in us. While it is true that God wants us to get along with others—"If it is possible, as far as it depends on you, live at peace with everyone" (Romans 12:18)—some of us carry that too far. Many of us, in fact, are so afraid of losing the approval of others that we don't set proper boundaries and let people walk all over us. Keep in mind that Paul says, "If it is *possible*, as far as it depends on you . . ." With some people, especially those who are narcissistic, it *isn't* possible to get along, unless we sacrifice our integrity to do so.

Assessing Your Beliefs

Let's examine some of the traits of a people pleaser. Complete the following self-assessment inventory using the scale below to determine how strongly these people-pleasing traits apply to you. Make sure you respond to each statement in terms of how you actually *are* versus how you think *you should be*. Again, try to avoid using the neutral response (4) whenever possible.

1	2	3	4	5	6	7
Strongly Disagree			Neutral			Strongly Agree

_____   1. I rarely say no to others.

_____   2. I pretend to agree with everyone.

_____   3. I go to great lengths to avoid conflict.

_____   4. I fear negative emotions in others.

_____   5. I feel responsible for how others feel.

_____   6. I act like those around me.

_____   7. I hesitate to admit when my feelings are hurt.

_____   8. I'm easily impressed by others.

_____   9. I over-explain myself.

_____   10. I need external praise to feel good about myself.

_____   11. I apologize too often.

Look back through your answers and circle any statement you gave a *6* or *7*, as these responses suggest you tend to be too much of a people pleaser.

The TRUTH Model

Next, choose one of those statements and focus on that particular issue in your *TRUTH Journal*. For example, if you strongly agreed with the statement "I rarely say no to others," be on the lookout as you go through this lesson for an opportunity to say no when it would be appropriate to do so. Let's run this through the TRUTH model to drive it home:

T	R	U	T	H
Trigger Event	**Ruined Thoughts**	**Unhealthy Response**	**Truthful Thoughts**	**Healthy Response**
Coworker who lost his license due to a DUI asked to borrow my car.	*I can't say no to him—it would be rude and hurt his feelings.*	Felt resentful and was tempted to say yes when I didn't really want to and knew I shouldn't.	*It's okay to tell him no—especially given that he lost his license and isn't covered by my insurance.*	Still felt somewhat anxious but was able to say no.

Let's try another example. Assume you gave a *6* or *7* to the statement, "I pretend to agree with everyone." Here's how this might look in your *TRUTH Journal*:

T	R	U	T	H
Trigger Event	**Ruined Thoughts**	**Unhealthy Response**	**Truthful Thoughts**	**Healthy Response**
Friends discussing their political views, many of which I view as uninformed and shallow.	*I think they're wrong to view things the way they do!*	Felt anxious and kept my thoughts to myself while fuming inside.	*I don't agree with them, and it's okay to be honest and say what I think.*	Felt anxious but spoke honestly about how I view things, knowing they might not like what I had to say.

Playing to an Audience of One

As followers of Christ, we are to care about one thing and only one thing: *the approval of God*. Obviously, we aren't to purposely and sinfully antagonize other people, but neither are we to shrink back and be voiceless when interacting with them. Healthy relationships are to be as "iron sharpens iron" (Proverbs 27:17), and at times this will involve tension and conflict so everyone can grow to see reality more accurately and be as mature as possible.

But the bottom line is that we are to ultimately care about the approval of God. If God is displeased with something we felt (resentment, fear, bitterness), or thought

(*Bill is a stupid idiot*), and/or did (told Bill he is a stupid idiot), we need to care about His thoughts on the matter and do what He wants us to do to make a mid-course correction.

In light of this tendency to be a people pleaser, I want you to work today on addressing that natural bent by implementing some changes in how you interact with others. In the space provided below, write down some thoughts about how to relate to others without unhealthily seeking their approval or trying to please them. Be specific as to the person or people to whom you're referring and the context of the situation.

Situations Where I Need to Say "No" More Often

_____

_____

_____

_____

_____

_____

Situations Where I Need to Disagree with Others More Often

_____

_____

_____

_____

_____

_____

Situations Where I Need to Deal with Conflict Head-on

_____

_____

_____

_____

_____

_____

Situations Where I Need to Be Okay with People Having Negative Feelings Toward Me

_____

_____

_____

_____

_____

_____

_____

_____

Situations Where I Need to Take Responsibility for My Feelings

_____

_____

_____

_____

_____

_____

_____

_____

Situations Where I Need to Resist Taking Responsibility for What Others Feel

_____

_____

_____

_____

_____

_____

_____

_____

Situations Where I Need to Act Differently Than Those Around Me

_____

_____

_____

_____

_____

_____

_____

_____

Situations Where I Need to Let People Know I Feel Hurt

_____

_____

_____

_____

_____

Situations Where I Need to Be Impressed by People's Character and Not Their Success

_____

_____

_____

_____

_____

Situations Where I Need to Keep the Explanation for My Actions Short

_____

_____

_____

_____

_____

Situations Where I Need to Feel Good About Being an Image Bearer Rather Than Because of What Someone Thinks of Me

_____

_____

_____

_____

_____

Situations Where I Need to Apologize for What I Did Wrong

_____

_____

_____

_____

_____

_____

_____

_____

_____

If you truly care about pleasing God and not people, you are at times going to get some hurtful (and even hateful) reactions from others. When that happens, see it as an opportunity to "participate in the sufferings of Christ" (1 Peter 4:13). Jesus was the rejected cornerstone (see Matthew 21:42) and more than familiar with the emotional pain of being treated in a hateful manner. Those are difficult footsteps to follow as a Christian, but it's important to do so in order to avoid being a fair-weather fan of Christ. Like Christ, you are to please God the Father and aspire to have His approval. If the crowd hates you and treats you badly, so be it.

I don't mean to be a pest, but please make sure you're doing your *TRUTH Journal* and choosing a Bible verse or two at the end of each lesson to memorize and contemplate on meditatively.

Key Memory and Meditation Verses

Do not follow the crowd in doing wrong (Exodus 23:2).

Fear of man will prove to be a snare, but whoever trusts in the LORD will be kept safe (Proverbs 29:25).

"Teacher," they said, "we know you are a man of integrity and that you teach the way of God in accordance with the truth. You aren't swayed by others, because you pay no attention to who they are" (Matthew 22:16).

For they loved human praise more than praise from God (John 12:43).

Am I now trying to win the approval of human beings, or of God? Or am I trying to please people? If I were still trying to please people, I would not be a servant of Christ (Galatians 1:10).

We are not trying to please people but God, who tests our hearts (1 Thessalonians 2:4).

Contemplative Prayer
(to be read slowly, meditatively, and repeatedly)

Heavenly Father,

I pray for Your help to overcome my fear of others and to simply focus on pleasing You each day. Help me to learn to say no to others when appropriate, disagree with people when it is right to do so, and head into conflict when it is necessary. Help me to stay calm when people have negative emotions toward me, to not take responsibility for how others feels toward me, to refuse to act like others when it is wrong to do so, and to be willing to let others know when I feel hurt by their actions.

Father, I also request that you help me to not be easily impressed by others —especially when their accomplishments are worldly and ego-driven, to avoid over-explaining my actions, to not seek human praise to feel good about myself, and to only apologize when I have done something wrong. Help me to avoid seeking the approval of others rather than You so that I will not violate my integrity in terms of who you meant me to be. I want to quit playing to the crowd and only play to an audience of One—to You, Father.

In the precious and holy name of Your Son, Jesus Christ. Amen.

THERE'S NO GAIN
WITHOUT PAIN

*Delaying gratification is a process of scheduling the pain
and pleasure of life in such a way as to enhance the
pleasure by meeting and experiencing the pain first and
getting it over with. It is the only decent way to live.*

M. SCOTT PECK

*We also glory in our sufferings, because we
know that suffering produces perseverance;
perseverance, character; and character, hope.*

ROMANS 5:3–4

We all have a natural inclination to run from pain and toward pleasure—
something psychologists call the "pleasure principle." Unfortunately, when
we choose to run from our painful day-to-day problems, we only see them get worse
over time. Furthermore, this fallen bent to seek gratification instead of face painful
things head-on becomes especially problematic in three areas of life: (1) the *lust of the
flesh*, (2) the *lust of the eyes*, and (3) the *pride of life* (see 1 John 2:15–17). The enemy
will often tempt us in these three areas to run from pain and toward things that will
give us immediate relief—to the point that they can become addictions.

The Temptations

The purpose of this lesson is to encourage you to be honest with yourself about these three areas of instant gratification and to do something about them. We will begin by assessing how these areas of temptation damage your life when you indulge them.

Lust of the Flesh

The *lust of the flesh* has to do with deriving physical gratification from sinful activities (overeating, getting drunk, engaging in immoral sexual activity, taking illegal drugs). In the space below, write down specific ways you have given in to this temptation and what the cost has been of doing so. For instance, under *Example*, you might write, "I eat a lot of fried food," and under *Damage to My Life*, you might write, "Have gained thirty pounds and my cholesterol level is too high." Now, I don't want you to shame or condemn yourself in writing these down, but you do need to be honest about what you are doing to indulge the lust of the flesh and what the cost of doing so has been in damaging the quality of your life.

Example #1: _____

Damage to My Life:

_____

_____

_____

Example #2: _____

Damage to My Life:

_____

_____

_____

Example #3: _____

Damage to My Life:

_____

_____

_____

Lust of the Eyes

The *lust of the eyes* has to do with deriving pleasure from longingly and covetously looking at something or someone that is beautiful or attractive to you (lustfully looking at an attractive person, coveting a material possession like a fancy car, desiring a more opulent home). In this section, identify the people and/or material possessions you have covetously longed for and what the cost has been for doing so. For instance, under *Example*, you might write, "I covet designer handbags that cost a fortune," and under *Damage to My Life*, you might write, "I spent money I didn't have and built up my credit card debt." Again, don't shame or condemn yourself for the struggles you have . . . just admit to having them.

Example #1: _____

Damage to My Life:

_____

_____

_____

Example #2: _____

Damage to My Life:

_____

_____

_____

Example #3: _____

Damage to My Life:

_____

_____

_____

Pride of Life

The *pride of life* has to do with deriving pleasure from being seen in other people's eyes as great, awesome, powerful, and more important or special than those around you. Some examples might include trying to make a name for yourself for self-glorifying reasons, making false accusations about others to make yourself look better, or obtaining a position of power to puff up your ego. In a word, sinful *pride* relates to how you want others to see you.

In this section, take a few minutes to write down where you find yourself giving in to pride of life and what the cost has been. For instance, under *Example*, you might write "Made a false accusation against a friend to make myself look better" and under *Damage to My Life*, you might write "Permanently damaged my relationship with that person and wrongly harmed their reputation." Avoid shaming yourself for doing these things, but make sure you take full responsibility for having done them.

Example #1: _____

Damage to My Life:

_____

_____

_____

Example #2: _____

Damage to My Life:

_____

_____

_____

Example #3: _____

Damage to My Life:

_____

_____

_____

Learning to Delay Gratification

The following is a list of several ways you can break free from areas of instant gratification in your life. These are all ways you can show God you're serious about repenting of the sinful and destructive things you've allowed into your life. In the space below, write down what you *have* done in each of these areas to overcome a particular temptation. In some cases, you will find you *haven't* done these things yet, so take a minute to note those as well.

Acknowledge My Physical Body Is God's and Not Mine

_____

_____

_____

_____

_____

_____

_____

Acknowledge My Fallen Bent to Gratify My Flesh

_____

_____

_____

_____

_____

_____

_____

Admit I Don't Have Sufficient Personal Willpower to Overcome My Struggle

_____

_____

_____

_____

_____

_____

Dedicate My Physical Body to God, Especially the Parts I Struggle to Control

_____

_____

_____

_____

_____

_____

Ask the Holy Spirit for Help to Grow in Self-Control in Delaying Gratification

_____

_____

_____

_____

_____

_____

Join a Growth Group for Help

_____

_____

_____

_____

_____

Hopefully, you are still doing your *TRUTH Journal*. Today, use it to monitor where the lust of the flesh, the lust of the eyes, and the pride of life show up in the *U* column (Unhealthy Response) and what biblical thoughts in the second *T* column might lead you to cope with these temptations in a healthier manner. With God's help, you don't need to be discouraged about overcoming those areas of sin in your life, no matter how deeply embedded they may be.

Key Memory and Meditation Verses

Flee from sexual immorality. All others sins a person commits are outside the body, but whoever sins sexually, sins against their own body (1 Corinthians 6:18).

No temptation has overtaken you except what is common to mankind. And God is faithful; he will not let you be tempted beyond what you can bear. But when you are tempted, he will also provide a way out so you can endure it (1 Corinthians 10:13).

It is for freedom that Christ has set us free (Galatians 5:1).

You, my brothers and sisters, were called to be free. But do not use your freedom to indulge the flesh, rather serve one another humbly in love (Galatians 5:13).

I can do all this through him who gives me strength (Philippians 4:13).

His divine power has given us everything we need for a godly life through our knowledge of him who called us by his own glory and goodness. Through these he has given us his very great and precious promises, so that through them you may participate in the divine nature, having escaped the corruption in the world caused by evil desires (2 Peter 1:3–4).

Contemplative Prayer

(to be read slowly, meditatively, and repeatedly)

Heavenly Father,

I'm so prone to indulge the lust of my flesh, the lust of my eyes, and the pride of life that resides in my physical body. Left to my own devices, my life would spin completely out of control, cause my own ruin, and hurt those who love me. Today, I ask that You help me to acknowledge that my physical body is Yours and not mine, that I have a natural bent to gratify my flesh, and that I don't have the ability to turn things around in my own power.

Father, help me to also recognize my body is Yours to do with what You will, to rely on the Holy Spirit's authority and power to help me develop self-control, and to seek support and encouragement from other fellow strugglers to overcome the struggle I have with sin. I pray that I would not minimize my struggle with these three kinds of sin or rationalize them in light of how others live their lives. Help me to experience godly sorrow that leads to repentance about my sins so I can experience the freedom Christ came to help us experience.

In the precious and holy name of Your Son, Jesus Christ. Amen.

LESSON 14

LOVE NEVER FAILS

Did I offer peace today? Did I bring a smile to someone's face?
Did I say words of healing? Did I let go of my anger and resentment?
Did I forgive? Did I love? These are the real questions.

HENRI NOUWEN

Love is patient, love is kind. It does not envy, it does not
boast, it is not proud. It does not dishonor others, it is not self-
seeking, it is not easily angered, it keeps no record of wrongs.
Love does not delight in evil but rejoices with the truth.

1 CORINTHIANS 13:4–6

As I mention in *The Lies We Believe*, the ancient Greeks believed love was multifaceted, and they had eight words to describe the different forms it could take. Two of these—*phila* (emotional fondness) and *eros* (sexual passion)—are the ones most people focus on today. But the Bible points to a higher form known as *agape*, which is a kind of love that actively pursues others, aims to meet their needs, is sacrificial, and attempts to foster other peoples' growth and maturity. Sadly, *agape* love is in short supply these days, as it is often overshadowed by the other lesser forms of love. In this lesson, we will turn our attention to how we can better express *agape* love to others in our lives.

The Three Not-Love Styles

There are three major ways we treat people in an unloving manner: (1) through *indifference/passivity*, (2) through *aggression/hostility*, and (3) through *passive-aggressiveness*. In the space below, write down specific examples of how you tend to mistreat others in each of these ways. Be specific in terms of the person to whom you act this way toward and the hurtful behavior that takes place in the way you treat him or her (some examples are listed below). Remember, honesty is the best policy in facing the things about you that need to change.

Situations Where I Was Indifferent/Passive Toward Others

(Examples: I rarely call my parents to see how they are doing; I infrequently pursue my spouse to meet her needs; I don't reach out to my friend often to see how he is doing.)

Situation #1: _____

_____

_____

_____

_____

Situation #2: _____

_____

_____

_____

_____

Situation #3: _____

_____

_____

_____

_____

Situations Where I Was Aggressive/Hostile Toward Others

(Examples: I sometimes lose my temper at work; I often say harsh things to the people in my life; I called my spouse a bad name yesterday during a fight.)

Situation #1: _____
_____
_____
_____
_____

Situation #2: _____
_____
_____
_____
_____

Situation #3: _____
_____
_____
_____
_____

Situations Where I Was Passive-Aggressive Toward Others

(Examples: I gave my boss a dirty look when he made a bad decision; I've been giving my friend the cold shoulder since she betrayed my trust; I did something I knew my spouse wouldn't like because I was angry at him.)

Situation #1: _____
_____
_____
_____
_____

Situation #2: _____

_____

_____

_____

_____

Situation #3: _____

_____

_____

_____

_____

Real Love

Let's now turn our attention to loving people *agape*-style. *Agape* love is multifaceted, and there is no simple definition of it. However, from my perspective, I find it has three important components: (1) it meets people's legitimate physical, emotional, and spiritual needs; (2) it involves treating people well (respectfully, civilly, decently, kindly); and (3) it fosters people's growth and maturity. Let me go more deeply into each of these components.

Meeting Physical, Emotional, and Spiritual Needs

God makes us with a body (our physical "earthsuit"), a soul (our mind, will, and emotions), and a spirit (the part of us that seeks meaning and purpose in life and can interact with God). God creates us in such a way that we are *needy* on all three levels:

- *Physical:* Our body needs air, food, and water to survive (and clothing and shelter as well).
- *Psychological:* Our soul (psyche) is needy in different ways, but we all have needs for attention, acceptance, appreciation, affirmation, affection, comfort, encouragement, respect, security, support, and understanding.
- *Spiritual:* We are spiritual beings who need meaning and purpose in life and the ability to interact with our Maker to live life properly.

When we think about what it means to *agape* love others, we need to keep these three areas of neediness in mind. If, as an act of our will, we meet a person's physical, psychological, or spiritual needs, we are loving them in an *agape* manner, whether they receive our love and or stiff-arm it. In the space below, write down three specific examples of how you can express this kind of *agape* love to another person.

Example #1: _____

_____

_____

_____

_____

Example #2: _____

_____

_____

_____

_____

Example #3: _____

_____

_____

_____

_____

Treating Other People Well

Agape love also involves *treating people well*. As the apostle Paul wrote, "Love is patient, love is kind. It does not envy, it does not boast, it is not proud. It does not dishonor others, it is not self-seeking, it is not easily angered, it keeps no record of wrongs. Love does not delight in evil but rejoices with the truth. It always protects, always trusts, always hopes, always perseveres" (1 Corinthians 13:4–7). When we interact with people in an *agape*-loving manner, we treat them with respect, dignity, and civility as fellow image-bearers. When we are kind, honoring, and gracious toward others, we are treating them well and *agape*-loving them. With this in mind, write down three ways you can express this kind of *agape* love to another person.

Example #1: _____

_____

_____

_____

_____

Example #2: _____

_____

_____

_____

_____

Example #3: _____

_____

_____

_____

_____

Foster Other People's Growth and Maturity

Finally, being an *agape*-loving person means looking for opportunities to help people grow and mature. We can foster people's growth in a number of different ways, from helping them to acquire a deeper and theologically solid understanding of important subject matters, to having open and safe discussions about things with which they struggle, to holding them accountable for making much-needed changes in their lives. When we aren't engaged in trying to help people mature, we are being unloving because we are not leaving them better off. *Agape* love is always aimed at facilitating the growth of others. In the space below, write down three ways you can express this kind of *agape* love to another person.

Example #1: _____

_____

_____

_____

_____

Example #2: _____

_____

_____

_____

_____

Example #3: _____

_____

_____

_____

_____

Always keep in mind that when you try to *agape* love others, it represents an effort on your part to open yourself up to be a conduit of *God's love.* When you love people in the three ways we just covered, you are obeying the second greatest commandment to "love your neighbor as yourself" (Mark 12:31). God *is* love (see 1 John 4:8), and any time you treat another person in an *agape*-loving manner, it is actually God working through you to love those who bear His image. God is the source of all the *agape* love expressed on the planet, so it's important to always give Him credit for working through you to *agape* love others well.

As we close this lesson, I don't want to be a nag, but I want to remind you to keep on doing your *TRUTH Journal.*

Key Memory and Meditation Verses

"For even the Son of Man did not come to be served, but to serve, and to give his life as a ransom for many" (Mark 10:45).

If I speak in the tongues of men or of angels, but do not have love, I am only a resounding gong or a clanging cymbal (1 Corinthians 13:1).

Love is patient, love is kind. It does not envy, it does not boast, it is not proud. It does not dishonor others, it is not self-seeking, it is not easily angered, it keeps no record of wrongs. Love does not delight in evil but rejoices with the truth (1 Corinthians 13:4–6).

Praise be to the God and Father of our Lord Jesus Christ, the Father of compassion and the God of all comfort, who comforts us in all our troubles, so that we can comfort those in any trouble with the comfort we ourselves receive from God (2 Corinthians 1:3–4).

Suppose a brother or a sister is without clothes and daily food. If one of you says to them, "Go in peace; keep warm and well fed," but does nothing about their physical needs, what good is it? (James 2:15–16).

If anyone has material possessions and sees a brother or sister in need but has no pity on them, how can the love of God be in that person? Dear children, let us not love with words or speech but with actions and in truth (1 John 3:17–18).

Contemplative Prayer
(to be read slowly, meditatively, and repeatedly)

Heavenly Father,

If I say I love You but don't love people, I prove myself to be a liar. Please help me to turn away from treating others in an unloving manner by isolating and withdrawing from them, attacking and being aggressive toward them, or being passive-aggressive in how I treat them. I know that I desperately need Your love to flow through me toward others by serving their needs better, treating them with greater respect and civility, and doing whatever I can to foster their growth and maturity.

Father, without your love flowing through me toward others, I am nothing but a resounding gong or a clanging cymbal. Please help me to be a conduit of Your love to the hurting people I encounter each day—the people You love with every fiber of Your being.

In the precious and holy name of Your Son, Jesus Christ. Amen.

IT'S NOT ALL ABOUT YOU

Half the harm that is done in this world is due to people who want to feel important. They don't mean to do harm. . . . Or they do not see it, or they justify it because they are absorbed in the endless struggle to think well of themselves.

T. S. ELIOT

But mark this: There will be terrible times in the last days. People will be lovers of themselves, lovers of money, boastful, proud, abusive, disobedient to their parents, ungrateful, unholy.

2 TIMOTHY 3:1–2

As children, we come into the world with a prewired tendency to focus on ourselves and our needs—something psychologists refer to as a "healthy narcissism." If our physical and psychological needs are met as children, we have a better shot at growing out of our narcissism and being respectful of the fact there are other people on the planet whose needs are just as important as ours. If we are mistreated growing up, we have a harder time letting go of our narcissism and can end up focusing too much on ourselves and on others meeting our needs.

Most of us have a mixture of healthy narcissism (an appropriate concern about ourselves and our valid needs being met) and unhealthy narcissism (an overly strong sense of self-centeredness and entitlement about our needs being met). God calls us to live to the former and die to the latter. So, in this lesson, we will focus on dying to our *unhealthy* narcissism and fulfilling the biblical challenge to "put off [the] old self, which is being corrupted by its deceitful desires" (Ephesians 4:22). To do this, we will begin by assessing the degree to which our narcissism is unhealthy, make the decision to turn away from it, and then ask God to help us be more selfless and loving toward others.

Assessing Your Beliefs

Remember that each of us is narcissistic to some degree. However, when our narcissism runs amuck, we will stand out like a sore thumb and be a wrecking ball in our relationships. To determine the degree of unhealthy narcissism in your life, complete the following self-assessment using the scale provided below. Again, make sure you answer in terms of how you really *are* versus how you think you *should be* along these various traits. As always, avoid using the neutral response (*4*) as much as possible.

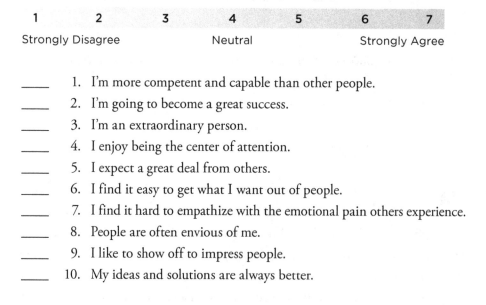

1	2	3	4	5	6	7
Strongly Disagree			Neutral			Strongly Agree

_____ 1. I'm more competent and capable than other people.

_____ 2. I'm going to become a great success.

_____ 3. I'm an extraordinary person.

_____ 4. I enjoy being the center of attention.

_____ 5. I expect a great deal from others.

_____ 6. I find it easy to get what I want out of people.

_____ 7. I find it hard to empathize with the emotional pain others experience.

_____ 8. People are often envious of me.

_____ 9. I like to show off to impress people.

_____ 10. My ideas and solutions are always better.

Circle any statement to which you gave a *6* or *7*, as these responses indicate you lean in the direction of an unhealthy narcissism on that particular issue. Note that this is not a scientifically validated questionnaire, but it can give you a sense of where you tend to be narcissistic in how you think about yourself and others. You will want to monitor the statements to which you gave a high rating in order to allow God to help you die to your old (narcissistic) self and live to the new (non-narcissistic) self as a follower of Christ.

The TRUTH Model

Next, I want you to focus on any issue of unhealthy narcissism in your life by using your *TRUTH Journal* to record events when they rear their ugly heads. Specifically, I want you to be on the lookout for when you feel bitter, resentful, or overly angry when reacting to a trigger event—and then whether you mentally filtered that event through narcissistic ways of looking at life. Let me give you a few examples.

T	R	U	T	H
Trigger Event	**Ruined Thoughts**	**Unhealthy Response**	**Truthful Thoughts**	**Healthy Response**
Someone cut in front of me in line at a movie theater.	*Boy, that person has a lot of nerve! Who does he think he is? Jerk!*	Felt my heart begin to race, became angry and resentful, gave him a dirty look when he caught my eye.	*The person was wrong to do that. It isn't a big deal. I'm not going to let it ruin the movie.*	Took a deep breath, felt a little calmer, and resumed talking with my friend.
Had a lot to do and parked in a handicap spot so I could be closer to the store I was entering.	*It's okay to park here. I'll be in and out in a jiffy. No one will notice or even care.*	Felt a tiny knot in my stomach, got out of my car, and started walking toward the storefront.	*It's not okay to park there. I've got enough time to repark—and even if I didn't, it's not okay to park in a handicap spot.*	Took a deep breath, got back in my car, and parked in a non-handicap spot.
Got bad service at an expensive restaurant.	*As expensive as this place is, I deserve much better service than this!*	Got angry and bitter, gave the manager a piece of my mind, went back to my table and stewed about it.	*The service could have been better, but I shouldn't have treated the manager like I did. I need to apologize.*	Took a deep breath, calmed down, apologized to the manager, and had an enjoyable meal.

Remember, it is healthy to *appropriately* look out for yourself in life and be assertive when things aren't the way they are supposed to be. However, you need to make sure you don't cross over the line and treat people badly when they do things you don't like.

Moving Away from Your Narcissism

We are always going to struggle with some degree of unhealthy narcissism in life, but God can help us weaken it over time if we cooperate with Him in the endeavor. As we discussed in *The Lies We Believe*, there are four ways God can help us become less malignantly narcissistic over time: (1) aim to serve, not be served; (2) value others more highly than ourselves; (3) think accurately about ourselves (humbly); and (4) submit to one another. Write down some concrete things you can do in each of these areas to die to that part of yourself that is too me-me-me-ish. Be specific as to the action you need to take and who you need to take it toward.

Ways I Can Meet the Needs of Others

_____

_____

_____

_____

_____

_____

_____

Ways I Can Value Others More Highly Than Myself

_____

_____

_____

_____

_____

_____

_____

Ways I Can Have a More Accurate View of Myself and Others

_____

_____

_____

_____

_____

_____

Ways I Can Appropriately Submit to Others

_____

_____

_____

_____

_____

_____

_____

Ways I Can Let Others Be the Center of Attention

_____

_____

_____

_____

_____

_____

Ways I Can Help Others Succeed

_____

_____

_____

_____

_____

_____

Ways I Can Express Empathy for the Emotional Pain Others Experience

_____

_____

_____

_____

_____

Ways I Can Stop Taking Advantage of Others

_____

_____

_____

_____

_____

Unhealthy narcissism is a form of soul cancer—something that will psychologically and spiritually eat us alive and cause harm to others along the way. For this reason, we need to make sure our focus is on serving others rather than being served, value others more highly than ourselves (even though we are all equally valuable in God's eyes), see ourselves accurately in terms of what our strengths and weaknesses are, and submit (in a healthy manner) to others as we co-labor through life. There is no other sane, non-narcissistic path in life.

Key Memory and Meditation Verses

"Whoever wants to become great among you must be your servant, and whoever wants to be first must be your slave—just as the Son of Man did not come to be served, but to serve, and to give his life as a ransom for many" (Matthew 20:26–28).

"Whoever wants to be my disciple must deny themselves and take up their cross daily and follow me. For whoever wants to save their life will lose it, but whoever loses their life for me will save it" (Luke 9:23–24).

Do not think of yourself more highly than you ought, but rather think of yourself with sober judgment, in accordance with the faith God has distributed to each of you (Romans 12:3).

You were taught, with regard to your former way of life, to put off your old self, which is being corrupted by its deceitful desires (Ephesians 4:22).

In humility value others above yourselves, not looking to your own interests but each of you to the interests of the others (Philippians 2:3–4).

God opposes the proud but shows favor to the humble (James 4:6).

Contemplative Prayer
(to be read slowly, meditatively, and repeatedly)

Heavenly Father,

I battle self-centeredness each and every day of my life. I often interact with others in a way designed to prop up my own ego and glorify myself. Only You are worthy of honor and glory, but I often lose sight of that fact in the way I approach others. Please help me to turn away from thinking that I am more competent and capable than others, that I am going to be a great earthly success, or that I am an extraordinary person who deserves to be the center of attention. Help me not to expect too much from others, or selfishly pursue what I want to get out of people, or refuse to empathize with other people's pain.

Father, help me to stop thinking that others are envious of me, or that I need to show off to impress people, or that my ideas and solutions are always better than those of others. In a word, please help me to quit going through life narcissistically and making everything about me. Help me to die to self, put others ahead of myself, and seek to serve rather than be served. I want to experience the joy and peace of self-forgetfulness and strive each and every day to leave others better off.

In the precious and holy name of Your Son, Jesus Christ. Amen.

LIFE IS DIFFICULT

*Don't pray for an easy life, pray for the
strength to endure a difficult one.*

BRUCE LEE

*"I have told you these things, so that in me you may
have peace. In this world you will have trouble."*

JOHN 16:33

Problems are woven into the fabric of life. The crucial issue, from a psychological health perspective, is whether we are going to face our problems when they come up or avoid them. If we face problems head-on, we can grow into more mature people and experience greater emotional health. However, if we avoid our problems, we won't mature as much and will struggle with a greater degree of emotional problems. Every day, we stand at the fork in the road between facing and avoiding our problems. The choice we make will significantly impact our emotional, relational, and spiritual health.

In this lesson, we are going to identify some of the internal and external problems we face in life and challenge ourselves to make a decision to tackle them head-on rather than run from them. In making the decision to face our problems, we are making a decision to be emotionally healthy people who grow and mature as our lives unfold.

Listing Your Problems

External problems can include major events such as the death of a loved one, significant financial challenges, severe marital discord, difficult issues at work, deteriorating health of a loved one, trouble with in-laws, and a change in our living situation. They can also include smaller "hassles" such as misplacing things, preparing meals, having to wait in lines, or having too many responsibilities or social obligations.

Internal problems of a major nature include serious psychiatric problems such as psychosis, personality disorders, post-traumatic stress disorders, depression, addictions, or clinically significant mood issues. They can also include hassles of a more minor nature like impatience, moodiness, loss of confidence, struggles with self-control, or being a tad too critical of others.

Evaluating External Problems

In the spaces provided below, write down some of your external problems (whether major or minor), what you are doing about them, and what you need to do about them if you are currently *not* facing them. Try to be as specific as possible when describing the problem and how you are trying to resolve it. Don't be afraid to admit if you are not doing anything to face a particular problem or if you are dealing with it in an unhealthy way. Honesty is the best policy.

External Problem #1: _____

What I'm Doing About It:

_____

_____

_____

What I Need to Do About It:

_____

_____

_____

External Problem #2: _____

What I'm Doing About It:

_____

_____

_____

What I Need to Do About It:

_____

_____

_____

External Problem #3: _____

What I'm Doing About It:

_____

_____

_____

What I Need to Do About It:

_____

_____

_____

Evaluating Internal Problems

Next, in the spaces provided below, write down some of your internal problems (whether major or minor), what you are doing about them, and what you need to do about them if you are currently *not* facing them. Try to be as specific as possible when describing the problem and how you are trying to resolve it. Again, don't be afraid to admit if you are not doing anything to face a particular problem or if you are dealing with it in an unhealthy way.

Internal Problem #1: _____

What I'm Doing About It:

_____

_____

_____

What I Need to Do About It:

_____

_____

_____

Internal Problem #2: _____

What I'm Doing About It:

_____

_____

_____

What I Need to Do About It:

_____

_____

_____

Internal Problem #3: _____

What I'm Doing About It:

_____

_____

_____

What I Need to Do About It:

_____

_____

_____

The Right Attitudinal Stuff

A major theme of *The Lies We Believe* is that your attitude about a difficult situation is far more important than the situation itself. In the book I told the story of Viktor Frankl, a captive in a Nazi concentration camp during World War II, who concluded it was the prisoners' *attitude* that determined how well or poorly they coped with their horrific situation. When it comes to your attitude, there are four important ways you can think about your problems: (1) you can view trials as an opportunity to grow, (2) you can choose to believe God is sovereign and see the positive in your situation, (3) you can tell God what you need, and (4) you can express gratitude in spite of the situation. In light of the external and internal problems you mentioned above, write how you can filter your thoughts through each of these four mindsets.

Mindset #1: How I Can See My Problems as an Opportunity to Grow

_____

_____

_____

_____

_____

_____

_____

**Mindset #2: Positive Things I Can Couple
with My Current Problems**

_____

_____

_____

_____

_____

_____

_____

Mindset #3: Help I Can Ask God to Give Me

_____

_____

_____

_____

_____

_____

_____

_____

Mindset #4: Ways I Can Thank God for His Help

_____

_____

_____

_____

_____

_____

_____

_____

Whenever problems come into your life, you have to make sure you see them as a chance to grow into a healthier person. It's important to couple them with the blessings you enjoy, ask God for help (rather than try to face them alone), and express gratefulness throughout the experience that He not only cares about what you are going through but is doing everything He can to help you handle it well. Attitude truly is everything . . . especially when it comes to dealing with the difficult problems you will experience in life.

Key Memory and Meditation Verses

"I have told you these things, so that in me you will have peace. In this world you will have trouble. But, take heart! I have overcome the world" (John 16:33).

No temptation has overtaken you except what is common to mankind. And God is faithful, he will not let you be tempted beyond what you can bear. But when you are tempted, he will also provide a way out so that you can endure it (1 Corinthians 10:13).

For our light and momentary troubles are achieving for us an eternal glory that far outweighs them all (2 Corinthians 4:17).

Do not be anxious about anything, but in every situation, by prayer and petition, with thanksgiving, present your requests to God. And the peace of God, which transcends all understanding, will guard your hearts and minds in Christ Jesus (Philippians 4:6).

Rejoice always, pray continually, give thanks in all circumstances; for this is God's will for you in Christ Jesus (1 Thessalonians 5:16–18).

Consider it pure joy, my brothers and sisters, whenever you face trials of many kinds, because you know that the testing of your faith produces perseverance (James 1:2)

Contemplative Prayer
(to be read slowly, meditatively, and repeatedly)

Heavenly Father,

You make it clear that in this world, difficult and painful problems will come my way. You also make it clear that when those problems come, You want me to face them rather than avoid them. Father, I'm so prone to run from my problems because I don't want to experience the pain involved in dealing with them. I desperately need Your help to courageously deal with the challenges of life.

Please help me to see my problems as a chance to grow, as an opportunity to acknowledge the good things that are still true in my life, as a time to turn to You for help, and as an opportunity to thank You for helping me get through the tough times. Help me to have a radical change in my thinking about my problems so that rather than avoid them I see them as a chance to share in the sufferings your Son went through—and to grow to be more like Him in the way I respond.

In the precious and holy name of Your Son, Jesus Christ. Amen.

ACCEPT WHAT YOU CAN'T CHANGE, CHANGE WHAT YOU CAN

God, give me the grace to accept with serenity the things that cannot be changed, courage to change the things which should be changed, and the wisdom to distinguish the one from the other.

REINHOLD NIEBUHR

Do you know how God controls the clouds and makes his lightning flash?

JOB 37:15

Many things are out of our control in life. Some of us struggle to accept this and try to exert control over people and circumstances in ways that are unhealthy and inappropriate. We end up being like Martha in the Bible, who was distracted by the preparations that had to be made when Jesus came for a visit and ended up being "worried and upset about many things." Her sister, Mary, on the other hand, chose "what is better" and sat at the Lord's feet listening to what he said—and, in so doing, was relatively calm and peaceful (see Luke 10:38–42).

To put it another way, we all have a control freak inside of us that tends to get sideways with the world when it doesn't act the way we want it to act. In this lesson, we will begin by assessing the degree to which we struggle with trying to control those things in life that we can't control. We will then turn our attention to working on accepting what we cannot change and changing what we can. First, let's self-assess.

How Much of a Martha Are You?

The traits related to being a control freak are on a continuum from "not really that way much at all" to "I'm super-controlling and trying to run the universe." Take a few minutes to fill out the questionnaire below to assess where you fall. Remember, be completely honest in your answers, resist answering in the "correct" way, and avoid using the neutral response (4).

1	2	3	4	5	6	7
Strongly Disagree			Neutral			Strongly Agree

_____ 1. I frequently correct and criticize other people.

_____ 2. I think I'm the only one who knows how to do things right.

_____ 3. I rarely admit when I'm wrong.

_____ 4. I don't believe others can do things on their own and that they need constant supervision and guidance.

_____ 5. I get angry when people don't hear my input first before making a decision.

_____ 6. I believe I know what is best for others.

_____ 7. I hate to delegate and am not a good team player.

_____ 8. I don't trust the judgement of others.

_____ 9. I can't handle criticism.

_____ 10. I have trouble hearing other people's points of view.

_____ 11. I assume a task is going to fail without my input.

_____ 12. I am extremely hard to please.

Look back through your answers and circle the statements you gave a *6* or *7*, as these responses suggest areas where you might struggle with being a control freak. Next, we will turn our attention to what you need to work on to overcome any of these unhealthy bents.

Addressing the Martha Inside You

Before we go any farther, I want to remind you that Martha dearly loved Jesus, was one of His closest friends, and was trying to be a hospitable host to Him and His followers on the day this infamous story took place. So, while you need to work on not being a control freak, you don't want to ignore the fact it is people like you who are often the ones operating at a high level of competency and productivity. That being said, in the spaces provided below, I want you to go through the twelve statements above and write down where you need to move in the *opposite* direction in your interpersonal relationships. Be specific about the person/people involved and how you need to adjust/ change your behavior so you can be less controlling.

**Situation #1: Where I Need to Stop
Criticizing and Correcting Others**

_____
_____
_____
_____
_____
_____
_____
_____

**Situation #2: Where I Need to Listen to
Others and Value How They Think**

_____
_____
_____
_____
_____
_____
_____
_____

Situation #3: Where I Need to Admit I Was Wrong

_____

_____

_____

_____

_____

**Situation #4: Where I Need to Trust Others
Don't Need My Supervision or Guidance**

_____

_____

_____

_____

_____

**Situation #5: Where I Need to Let People
Make Decisions Without My Input**

_____

_____

_____

_____

_____

**Situation #6: Where I Need to Trust People
Know What Is Best for Themselves**

_____

_____

_____

_____

_____

Situation #7: Where I Need to Delegate and Be a Better Team Player

_____

_____

_____

_____

_____

_____

Situation #8: Where I Need to Trust the Judgment of Others

_____

_____

_____

_____

_____

_____

Situation #9: Where I Need to Ask for Input and Correction

_____

_____

_____

_____

_____

_____

**Situation #10: Where I Need to Listen Better
to Other People's Point of View**

_____

_____

_____

_____

_____

_____

**Situation #11: Where I Need to Assume a Task
Is Going to Succeed Without My Input**

_____

_____

_____

_____

_____

_____

_____

_____

**Situation #12: Where I Need to Lower My
Standards and Be Easier to Please**

_____

_____

_____

_____

_____

_____

_____

_____

Don't worry if you couldn't come up with an example for every situation. Just continue to work on being aware of those situations where you need to practice anti-controlling behavior. In this way, you will be able to show respect to others when it comes to their talents and abilities and be able to support their way of dealing with a given challenge or problem.

Addressing Your Controlling Ways

If you have spent your life trying to control others, you have some amends to make to those you have hurt along the way. In this next section, I want to guide your steps through this much-needed time of relational repentance.

Step #1: Acknowledge God Is in Control

Acknowledge to God that He is in control of the universe—and you are not. Ask God to forgive You for any times you have questioned His sovereignty over all things and have gotten ahead of Him in trying to control things that are only His to control.

_____

_____

_____

_____

_____

_____

Step #2: Ask for Discernment About What You Can Control

Ask God to help you be more discerning about what you can control in life. In these areas where you can exert control (such as how you respond to difficult situations or temptations), ask God to empower your efforts. For those areas you can't control, ask God to help you turn them back over to Him and get out of His way in dealing with it.

_____

_____

_____

_____

_____

_____

Step #3: Write Down Ways to Influence Others

God doesn't want you to control others, but He also doesn't want you to go "radio silent" and not share your experiences about life. In fact, it is important for you to take what you have learned and pass it along to others so they can make wiser decisions and be more productive. To this end, write down ways you can influence others rather than control them.

_____

_____

_____

_____

_____

_____

Step #4: Come Up with an Action Plan

Acknowledging that you need to change your controlling ways is a nice start, but now you need to take the next step to generate and execute a plan on how to become different over time. In the space below, write down an action-oriented plan for how you can work collaboratively with God to change the way you are being controlling toward others.

_____

_____

_____

_____

_____

Step #5: Apologize to the People You've Tried to Control

When you try to control others, you treat them in a dishonoring and disrespectful manner because you deny they are independent human beings with free will who do not answer to you. For this reason, it's important to ask people to forgive you for trying to control them. In the space below, write down how you plan to accomplish this important step.

_____

_____

_____

_____

_____

Step #6: Implement Better Boundaries

Now consider the people in your life who are trying to control you and think of ways you can implement firmer, stiffer, tougher, clearer, or stronger boundaries with them. It's important to not only be assertive when others are trying to manipulate or exploit you but also to be open to talking things out with them if they are upset or bothered by your boundaries.

_____

_____

_____

_____

_____

Step #7: Cut Yourself Some Slack

Finally, you need to cut yourself some slack for being too controlling. Have compassion and empathy for the fact you are "worried and upset about many things" (which is bad enough!). Allow God's grace to help you choose the "better" path of resting at His feet, soaking Him in, and still productively getting things done.

_____

_____

_____

_____

_____

_____

_____

_____

Trying to control the universe is self-destructive and unhealthy. Instead, we need to recognize that God is "large and in charge" and humbly play our small part in His plan. Like Mary, we need to choose the "better thing" by getting to know Christ more intimately while still contributing our fair share in serving Him and the people around us.

Conclude your time by using your *TRUTH Journal* to track where you are trying to control people rather than serve and influence them. Keep asking God to help you play the right tapes in your mind when you get "worried and upset" that others are not acting the way you want. Over time, God will help you change from a controlling person into a person of influence—doing what you are supposed to do and challenging others to do the same.

Key Memory and Meditation Verses

Yours, LORD, is the greatness and the power and the glory and the majesty and the splendor, for everything in heaven and earth is yours. Yours, LORD, is the kingdom, you are exalted as head over all (1 Chronicles 29:11).

Our God is in heaven; he does whatever pleases him (Psalm 115:3).

So do not fear, for I am with you: do not be dismayed, for I am your God. I will strengthen you and help you: I will uphold you with my righteous right hand (Isaiah 41:10).

I am the Lord, the God of all mankind. Is there anything too hard for me? (Jeremiah 32:27).

"Come to me, all you who are weary and burdened, and I will give you rest" (Matthew 11:28).

Do not be anxious about anything, but in every situation, by prayer and petition, with thanksgiving, present your requests to God. And the peace of God, which transcends all understanding, will guard your hearts and minds in Christ Jesus (Philippians 4:6–7).

Contemplative Prayer
(to be read slowly, meditatively, and repeatedly)

Heavenly Father,

How often I find myself trying to control things that are not under my control and change others rather than work on changing myself! I have so much "Martha" in me, Father, and it leads me down the garden path of being resentful and bitter toward those who are not acting as I want them to act. Please help me to stop correcting and criticizing others, to admit when I'm wrong, and to believe others can do things on their own without my supervision and guidance. Help me to avoid getting angry when people don't seek my input, to not believe I always know what is best for others, and to being willing to delegate tasks to others.

Father, help me also to trust the judgment of others, to not respond defensively to corrective feedback, to being willing to listen attentively to other people's points of view, to not assume a task is going to fail without my involvement, and to not be overly hard to please. I don't want to treat people this way anymore—especially given that it gets in the way of me intimately relating to them in a loving and caring manner. Please help me to repent of my controlling ways and be a better team player for the cause of Christ.

In the precious and holy name of Your Son, Jesus Christ. Amen.

It's More Blessed to Give Than to Receive

*My father said there were two kinds of people
in the world: givers and takers. The takers
may eat better, but the givers sleep better.*

MARLO THOMAS

It is more blessed to give than to receive.

ACTS 20:35

Takers and *givers*. Where do you fall on the spectrum? Do you find yourself being more prone to *take* or more prone to *give*? Or, like most people, do you find that you are a mixture of the two? In life, there are times when you need to be in give-mode and put the needs of others ahead of your own. But there are also times you need to be in take-mode and let others give to you. The healthier the balance you can strike on this issue, the healthier person you will be. In this lesson, we will do some digging into this matter of giving and taking. Let's start off by assessing what kind of *unhealthy* taker you can be at times.

Three Kinds of Unhealthy Takers

As I discussed in *The Lies We Believe*, there are three kinds of unhealthy takers in life: (1) the give-to-get taker, (2) the equal taker, and (3) the full-blown taker. Let's go back and explore each of these three types of unhealthy relational styles a little further.

Relational Style #1: The Give-to-Get Taker

When we are in this mode, we give to people because we want something in return. For example, we may hold a door open for someone because we want a "thank you," or we may help someone move because we want them to help us paint our living room. In the space below, write down where you find yourself giving-to-get in the relationships you have.

_____

_____

_____

_____

_____

_____

_____

Relational Style #2: The Equal Taker

In this mode, we focus on whether things in a relationship are on equal footing. We keep a mental record of who has given what to whom and become resentful when we think we are giving more to others than they are giving to us. In the space below, write down when you tend to be an equal taker and get resentful when you are on the short end of the receiving stick.

_____

_____

_____

_____

_____

_____

_____

Relational Style #3: The Full-Blown Taker

In this mode, we take things with little (if any) intention of giving back and fundamentally exploit other people's goodwill toward us. In the space below, write down examples of when you have fallen into the full-blown taker mode in your relationships with others.

_____

_____

_____

_____

It's not fun to face these three relational styles, because they represent the ugly side of how all of us can act toward others. (I give you a big pat on the back for being willing to do so!) Now, let's turn our attention to how we can be healthy givers.

Five Traits of Healthy Givers

In *The Lies We Believe*, we explored five traits of those who are healthy givers: (1) they are service minded; (2) they are discerning; (3) they know their limits; (4) they give their time, talents, and treasures; and (5) they know how to receive. Let's now look at how we can "operationalize" those traits and incorporate them more into our interactions with others. As we do, we know that God, in His efforts to help us become more loving and mature, wants us to follow in the steps of Christ, who "did not come to be served, but to serve" (Matthew 20:28).

Trait #1: A Healthy Giver Looks for Ways to Serve

A healthy giver goes out into the world each day thinking, How can I serve others and leave them better off? They try to avoid the opposite thought—How can others serve me and leave me better off? In the space below, write down the way you tend to react when it comes to having the attitude of serving others or wanting them to serve you.

_____

_____

_____

_____

_____

Trait #2: A Healthy Giver Is Discerning About to Whom to Give

A healthy giver is wise enough to give to others based on them having legitimate needs. They do not give to others based on their desire to be selfish and exploitive. In the space below, write down (1) the ways you are currently giving to those with legitimate needs and (2) ways you are avoiding giving to those whose needs are illegitimate.

_____

_____

_____

_____

_____

Trait #3: A Healthy Giver Is Discerning About How Much to Give

We are all finite human beings with limitations in what we can offer to others. The healthy giver is thus wise about how much spiritual, psychological, and physical help to offer others. In the space below, write down (1) where you find yourself giving appropriately to others, and (2) where you find yourself giving too much of yourself.

_____

_____

_____

_____

_____

Trait #4: A Healthy Giver Gives Time, Talent, and Treasure

Healthy givers are loving to others by (1) giving of their time (especially along the lines of meeting their emotional needs), (2) sharing their talents and abilities (helping others in ways they are skilled or trained to help), and (3) meeting their physical/financial needs (providing for their basic survival needs and helping them get back up on their feet). In the space below, write down where you give your time, talents, and treasures to others in healthy ways.

_____

_____

_____

_____

_____

Trait #5: A Healthy Giver Allows Other to Give to Them

All too often, we either don't feel worthy of receiving from others, or we feel we shouldn't be on the receiving end of those who want to serve us. That attitude is not good for anybody, because it gets in the way of our needs being met and it gets in the way of the other person receiving the blessing of meeting those needs. In the space below, write down where you allow others to give to you in healthy and appropriate ways.

_____

_____

_____

_____

_____

_____

It's not easy to face the issue of giving and taking in life. Nevertheless, it is important to square up with those areas where you aren't giving to others when you need to do so, where you are giving to others when you shouldn't be, where you are taking from others in exploitive ways, and where you not allowing others to meet your needs because of insecurity (not feeling worthy) or pride (feeling self-sufficient).

Close by using your *TRUTH Journal* to monitor where your unhealthy taker, unhealthy giver, and unhealthy independence is showing up, and also what the right thoughts and actions need to be. Select a verse or two from the list below to memorize and meditate on that speaks to you about serving others in a Christlike manner—and allowing others to serve you.

Key Memory and Meditation Verses

Whoever is kind to the poor lends to the LORD, and he will reward them for what they have done (Proverbs 19:17).

"Whoever wants to become great among you must become your servant, and whoever wants to be first must become your slave—just as the Son of Man did not come to be served, but to serve, and to give his life as a ransom for many" (Matthew 20:26–28).

"The King will reply, 'Truly I tell you, whatever you did for one of the least of these brothers and sisters of mine, you did for me'" (Matthew 25:40).

Carry each other's burdens, and in this way you will fulfill the law of Christ (Galatians 6:2).

Rather, in humility value others above yourselves, not looking to your own interests but each of you to the interests of the others (Philippians 2:3–4).

God is not unjust; he will not forget your work and the love you have shown him as you have helped his people and continue to help them (Hebrews 6:10).

Contemplative Prayer
(to be read slowly, meditatively, and repeatedly)

Heavenly Father,

Your beloved Son came to serve, not to be served. Please help me to be more like Him. Help me to turn away from being a give-to-get taker, equal taker, or full-blown taker in my interactions with others. I need Your wisdom to be more discerning about to whom I should give, how much to give, and how much of the time, talents, and treasures You have given me to offer to them.

Father, I also pray for Your help to be more open to allowing people to serve me rather than give in to false notions of self-sufficiency. Help me to grow more comfortable in giving sacrificially rather than in ways that aren't costly. Help me to give of myself with no strings attached and not expect anything in return. Help me to pour myself out like a drink offering to a dry and thirsty world. Thank You for giving me Your precious Son—something I will never be able to repay. I pray for Your help to show my gratitude by putting myself under Your authority and serving who You want me to serve.

In the precious and holy name of your Son, Jesus Christ, Amen.

YOU ARE A PERSON OF GREAT WORTH

*We're all human, aren't we? Every human life
is worth the same, and worth saving.*

J. K. ROWLING

*I praise you because I am fearfully and
wonderfully made; your works are
wonderful, I know that full well.*

PSALM 139:14

All of us battle some degree of shame in our lives. Even those brimming with self-confidence—those who seem to have it all together—will battle shame in some areas of their lives. In this lesson, we will work on reducing our sense of shame and strengthening our sense of worth. To begin, let's examine the four faces of shame and do some self-assessment.

The Four Faces of Shame

Shame takes many forms. In *The Lies We Believe*, we explored four versions of malignant shame: (1) a sense of worthlessness, (2) a sense of being unworthy to love, (3) a sense of believing it's always our fault when things go wrong, and (4) a sense that it's not okay to be human. Let's review each of these cancerous types of shame and write about the degree to which they can cause damage to us and our interactions with others.

Malignant Shame #1: A Sense of Worthlessness

Some of us grew up believing that we were worthless, bad, good-for-nothing sinners in the hands of a righteous God who was disgusted with us. In the space provided below, write down any thoughts you have about yourself along these lines.

_____

_____

_____

_____

_____

Malignant Shame #2: A Sense of Being Unworthy to Love

Some of us have come to believe that because we have flaws and defects, we are unworthy of love from other people and from God. In the space below, write down any thoughts you have had along these lines.

_____

_____

_____

_____

_____

Malignant Shame #3: A Sense of It's Always Your Fault

Sometimes, our shame issues will show up in the form of believing that when a relationship goes bad, it's always our fault. When others are upset, we feel we were the ones who caused the problems and are the ones who needs to fix everything. In the space below, write down any thoughts you have had along these lines.

_____

_____

_____

_____

_____

Malignant Shame #4: A Sense of It Not Being Okay to Be Human

Finally, malignant shame can show up in the form of believing it's not okay to be a human being who makes a lot of mistakes. Self-condemnation is always near at hand, and when we mess up—especially if the mistake is significant—we beat ourselves up for it. In the space below, write down any thoughts you have had along these lines.

Ever since the fall of humankind, when Adam and Eve went from being "naked and unashamed" to "naked and ashamed" (see Genesis 2:25–3:10), the enemy has used these four *unbiblical* ways of thinking to shame us and keep us down. These ways of thinking generate strong feelings of sadness, despair, hopelessness, and self-hatred within us. And when toxic shame is running the show, we have a harder time getting close to God and others because we fundamentally don't feel worthy of having a loving, intimate relationship with anyone. So, in this next section, let's turn our attention to God's response to our shame issues and learn what He wants us to internalize about the way He views us.

God's Prescription for Shame

Regardless of the version of shame with which we struggle, God has the antidote. This is especially true when it comes to those of us who battle a deep-seated sense of shame from having done horrible things in the past. With this in mind, let's go through God's four-prescription approach to eradicating malignant shame so we can live healthier and fuller lives.

Prescription #1: Recognize Your Inherent Worth

Most of us tie our worth to our performance, and when our performance goes up and down, our sense of worth goes up and down with it. Yet the Bible is clear our worth comes from one thing only—being made by God in His image (see Genesis 1:26). In the Psalms we read, "You have made them a little lower than the angels and crowned them with glory and honor," and, "You created my inmost being; you knit me together in my mother's womb. I am fearfully and wonderfully made; your works are wonderful, I know that full well" (8:5; 139:13–14).

These and dozens of other passages in Scripture are meant to cleanse us of any feelings of worthlessness. We only play into the enemy's hands when we revert back to defining our worth the way the world does: through performance. In light of these teachings in Scripture, write down your thoughts on what it means to be an image bearer who is fearfully and wonderfully made, created a little lower than the angels, and a breathtaking work of God.

_____

_____

_____

_____

_____

_____

_____

_____

Prescription #2: Accept God's Unmeasurable Love and Unmerited Favor

Another way God tries to free us from the effects of malignant shame is by offering us a love that cannot be measured and grace that makes us righteous in His eyes. Regarding God's love, Paul wrote, "I pray that you, being rooted and established in love, may power, together with all the Lord's holy people, *to grasp how wide and long and high and deep is the love of Christ, and to know that his love surpasses knowledge*" (Ephesians 3:17–19, emphasis added). Regarding God's grace, Paul wrote, "For all have sinned and fall short of the glory of God, and all are *justified freely by his grace* through the redemption that came by Jesus Christ" (Romans 3:23–24, emphasis added).

Unfortunately, far too many of us spend our lives trying to *earn* God's love and *merit* His favor, when neither has anything to do with our good or bad actions while we're here. Instead, those of us who are God's children need to *accept* His amazing gifts and allow them to permanently destroy any scintilla of viewing ourselves through shame-based lenses. With this in mind, write down any thoughts you have about the unconditional love and unmerited favor that God has extended toward you.

_____

_____

_____

_____

_____

_____

_____

_____

Prescription #3: Acknowledge Your God-Wired Traits, Abilities, and Gifts

God also cleanses us of our shame by wiring into our souls many abilities, skills, talents, traits, passions, and interests. The fact that God, after creating human beings, stepped back and "saw all that He had made, and [said] it was *very* good" (Genesis 1:31, emphasis added), should permanently remove any feelings of shame within us. But even more, once we become followers of Christ, God equips us with a spiritual gift (or gifts) of some kind (see 1 Corinthians 12:4).

The apostle Paul writes that these spiritual gifts, given to us by the Holy Spirit, are to be used to "equip [God's] people for works of service, so that the body of Christ may be built up" (Ephesians 4:12). Given how God has made and equipped us, we need to go through life with our heads held high and recognize that we have wonderful things to offer others while we are here. In the space below, write down how knowing God "fearfully and wonderfully" created you as a unique masterpiece can set you free from toxic feelings of shame.

_____

_____

_____

_____

_____

_____

_____

Prescription #4: Believe That You Are an Heir of All That Is God's

There is one final reality that followers of Christ need to understand—something that should knock our socks off whenever the enemy tries to throw the fiery darts of toxic shame at us. When God adopts us into His family, we inherit *everything* He possesses. As Paul writes, "Now if we are children, then we are heirs—heirs of God and co-heirs with Christ, if indeed we share in his sufferings in order that we may also share in his glory" (Romans 8:17). When God adopts us as His children, we go from being paupers to being members of the Royal Family. Just think of that. *Everything* God possesses belongs to us . . . because we belong to Him.

Furthermore, this inheritance is one "that can never perish, spoil or fade" (1 Peter 1:4). What exactly is it that you inherit when you become a follower of Christ? In a word, *heaven*. You inherit the Eternal City. John writes in Revelation that he saw this Eternal City "prepared as a bride beautifully dressed for her husband" (21:2). He describes it as a place where God will "wipe every tear" from our eyes, where "the foundations of the city walls [are] decorated with every kind of precious stone," where "the great street of the city was of gold, as pure as transparent glass," and where there is no need for the sun or the moon, because "the glory of God gives it light, and the Lamb is its lamp" (verses 4, 19, 21, 23).

Can you wrap your mind around the fact that becoming a follower of Christ means the deed to heaven now has your name on it? In the space below, write down how this fact can set you free from the toxic and malignant effects of shame in your life.

_____

_____

_____

_____

_____

_____

_____

_____

_____

_____

_____

_____

So, the next time the father of lies tries to convince you that you are worthless, unworthy of love, the reason relationships go south, or not accepted because you make mistakes, don't believe a word of it. Instead, believe what God says about you—you are fearfully and wonderfully made in His image, created only a little lower than the angels, immeasurably loved, bathed in His unmerited favor and forgiveness, imbued with wonderful traits and abilities, supernaturally empowered with gifts for serving the body of Christ, and an heir who has received the keys to God's own Heavenly City. Yeah . . . believe that!

Key Memory and Meditation Verses

You have made them a little lower than the angels and crowned them with glory and honor (Psalm 8:5).

My frame was not hidden from you when I was made in the secret place, when I was woven together in the depths of the earth (Psalm 139:15).

For all have sinned and fall short of the glory of God, and all are justified freely by his grace through the redemption that came by Christ Jesus (Romans 3:23–24).

Now if we are children, then we are heirs—heirs of God and co-heirs with Christ, if indeed we share in his sufferings in order that we may also share in his glory (Romans 8:17).

I pray that you, being rooted and established in love, may have power, together with all the Lord's holy people, to grasp how wide and long and high and deep is the love of Christ, and to know this love that surpasses knowledge—that you may be filled to the measure of all the fullness of God (Ephesians 3:17–19).

In his great mercy he has given us a new birth into a living hope through the resurrection of Jesus Christ from the dead, and into an inheritance that can never perish, spoil or fade. This inheritance is kept in heaven for you (1 Peter 1:4).

Contemplative Prayer
(to be read slowly, meditatively, and repeatedly)

Heavenly Father,

Your Word tells us that shame and condemnation come from the enemy, not from You. Yet I have struggled throughout my life with feelings that I am worthless, unworthy of love, the cause of all relationship conflicts, and that it is not okay for me to be human and make mistakes. I find that if others don't shame and condemn me for my flaws and defects, I will often do it for them.

Father, I know that You created me in Your image and that I have inherent worth as a human being. I know that Your love for me is unmeasurable and that I am worthy of being loved as a result. I know that You have equipped me with talents and abilities and that I have something to offer the world. I know that at times when I experience conflict it is not my fault and is largely due to the other person mistreating me. I know that because I was born with a natural bent to sin, I am inevitably going to make mistakes, but that those mistakes do not separate me from Your love. And I know that You have adopted me into Your family and that I am now an heir of all that is Yours in heaven.

Father, help me to go from simply knowing these things to deeply believing them in the innermost part of my being. Thank You for all the things You do to help me break free from the shame and self-condemnation that I have experienced during my life. Thank You for your unmeasurable love, Your unmerited favor, and Your total forgiveness.

In the precious and holy name of Your Son, Jesus Christ. Amen.

THE WORLD OWES
YOU NOTHING

I'm here today to warn you: I want you to
watch out for the adversary. Guard yourself
from any spirit of entitlement.

CHARLES SWINDOLL

God opposes the proud but shows favor to the humble.

JAMES 4:6

Entitlement. We all have a case of it. To some degree, we all believe we are entitled to love, justice, employment, happiness, a spouse, children . . . and whatever else goes along with the "good life." We may express it in different ways—from "I deserve," to "I expect," to "I demand," to "I'm owed"—but those are just different ways of saying that deep down in our soul, we think we are entitled to everything we want during our brief time here on earth.

Our world seems to be getting worse in its sense of entitlement. It has gotten so bad that some people—though they haven't put much into making the world a better place—feel entitled to the world giving them the red-carpet treatment, as if they were God's gift to the planet. It is one thing for people to feel entitled to payback when they have worked hard, contributed a great deal, and left the world better off, but it's a whole different matter when people contribute little and still demand that life reward them handsomely.

In this lesson, we are going to go after that unhealthy part of our flesh that feels the world owes us something. After that, we are going to work on shifting from feeling entitled to *wanting* or *desiring* the things God has for us. But first, let's do a little self-assessment.

Your Entitlement in Relationships

Entitlement is a component of narcissism. For this reason, much of what we are going to cover will have a familiar ring to it, because it reflects a narcissistic attitude toward life that we covered in a previous lesson. However, in this lesson, I want you to think about the relationships you have where you tend to fall into a sense of entitlement and then write down *how you express this sense of entitlement in the way you interact* with those people.

Relationships Where I Tend to Make Everything About Me

_____

_____

_____

_____

Relationships Where Others See Me as a Manipulative Bully

_____

_____

_____

_____

Relationships Where I Take More Than I Give

_____

_____

_____

Relationships Where I Dominate and Bully Those Around Me

_____
_____
_____
_____
_____

Relationships Where I See Others as Competition

_____
_____
_____
_____
_____

Relationships Where I Step on Others

_____
_____
_____
_____
_____

Relationships Where I Place Unrealistic Demands on Others

_____
_____
_____
_____
_____

Relationships Where I Crave Attention and Admiration

_____
_____
_____
_____
_____

Relationships Where I Punish People Who Don't Give Me What I Want

_____

_____

_____

_____

Relationships Where I Have a Double Standard

_____

_____

_____

_____

Relationships Where I Lack Empathy for How Others Feel About My Actions

_____

_____

_____

_____

Relationships Where I Go to Any Means to Succeed in Getting What I Want

_____

_____

_____

_____

Relationships Where I Believe I Should Always Come First

_____

_____

_____

_____

Relationships Where I Feel Bitter and Resentful Toward Others

_____

_____

_____

_____

_____

_____

_____

_____

Evaluating Your Entitlement Issues

We're not quite done assessing the entitlement issues in your life. In the spaces provided below, write down the things you feel you are entitled to receive in life given what you know about yourself. The best way to do this is to ask yourself, *In what areas do I feel bitter and resentful that something didn't come my way?* Bitterness and resentment are the emotional "red flags" that indicate an underlying sense of entitlement, so use those emotions to assess where this entitlement has reared its ugly head in your life. In the space below, write down at least seven things to which you feel entitled (such as *love, fairness, appreciation, support, a promotion, a spouse, friends, loyalty, affirmation, respect, attention, people showing up on time, civility*). If you can't come up with at least seven, you're not being honest with yourself.

I feel entitled to _____

I feel entitled to _____

I feel entitled to _____

I feel entitled to _____

I feel entitled to _____

I feel entitled to _____

I feel entitled to _____

Now that you have a better understanding about the things to which you feel entitled, let's move on to what you need to do to overcome this deadly attitude.

Desire Versus Demand

This may sound like semantics, but the mindset to work on is *wanting* or *desiring* things in life, not *demanding* or feeling *entitled* to them. This difference is huge on an emotional level. If you demand or feel entitled to things, you will feel bitter and resentful when people don't give them to you. However, if you want or desire things, the worst you risk emotionally is feeling sad, disappointed, and hurt when they don't come your way. Metaphorically, bitterness and resentment are like cancer to the soul, whereas disappointment, hurt, and sadness are like the flu to your soul. These emotions don't feel good, but they won't kill you. Review the seven items you listed above to which you feel entitled to receive. Then, as simplistic as it may seem, put those items into the following sentences:

I want _____

I want _____

I want _____

I want _____

I want _____

I want _____

I want _____

In order to make progress in overcoming your entitlement issues, it is important to work on mentally switching from thinking you are *entitled* to things to thinking it is okay to *want* them. This one change in your attitude will help free you from feeling bitter and resentful to feeling disappointed, sad, and hurt. I encourage you to emotionally opt for the latter rather than the former, for God tells us in His Word to "get rid of all bitterness, rage and anger, brawling and slander, along with every form of malice" (Ephesians 4:31). Making the attitudinal shift from "I'm entitled to . . . " to "I want . . ." is a major step in that direction.

Your Desires Versus God's Desires

We're not quite out of the woods yet. The final item I want you to examine is whether what you want in life are the things God wants for you—in other words, whether your wants are biblical, moral, ethical, and proper. With that in mind, write down ten things you want in life that you are reasonably sure God wants for you as well. For example, you could write, "God wants me to have healthy relationships with others." What else falls into this category for you?

Things I Want in Life That God Wants for Me

1. _____
2. _____
3. _____
4. _____
5. _____
6. _____
7. _____
8. _____
9. _____
10. _____

Now turn your attention to the flip side of the coin. What are ten things you want in life that you are reasonably sure God *doesn't* want for you? For example, you could write, "God doesn't want me to be glorified here on earth." What else falls into this category for you?

Things I Want in Life That God Does *Not* Want for Me

1. _____
2. _____
3. _____
4. _____
5. _____
6. _____
7. _____
8. _____
9. _____
10. _____

Stay the course when it comes to moving away from that fallen part of you that feels entitled to certain things and moving toward the things God wants for you. Keep asking God to shift you from this toxic mindset to the humbler mindset of simply desiring those things. And keep your eyes open when it comes to whether you want the things that God wants for you. You don't want to be at cross purposes with God by pursuing things on earth that only the enemy wants you to have. Instead, desire what God wants for you . . . and you will find that He will do everything He can to make it happen.

Key Memory and Meditation Verses

*Take delight in the L*ORD*, and he will give you the desires of your heart* (Psalm 37:4).

Pride goes before destruction, a haughty spirit before a fall (Proverbs 16:18).

"For those who exalt themselves will be humbled, and those who humble themselves with be exalted" (Matthew 23:12).

Furthermore, just as they did not think it worthwhile to retain the knowledge of God, so God gave them over to a depraved mind, so that they do what ought not to be done (Romans 1:28).

Be completely humble and gentle; be patient, bearing with one another in love (Ephesians 4:2).

Get rid of all bitterness, rage and anger, brawling and slander, along with every form of malice (Ephesians 4:31).

Contemplative Prayer
(to be read slowly, meditatively, and repeatedly)

Heavenly Father,

I am prone to having a spirit of entitlement as I live my life. I find myself feeling entitled to being loved, having a good life, experiencing fairness and justice, receiving help and blessings—all the while knowing in my head that I am entitled to none of these things. I pray that You would help me repent of having an attitude of entitlement and that You would help me shift my thoughts to wanting and desiring the things in life that you want for me as well.

Father, Your Son came to earth as God-incarnate, yet He didn't exhibit a spirit of entitlement in His interactions with others. How much of an insult it must be when you see me feeling entitled to things when your Son didn't have that sense of entitlement. In a world that seems to feel entitled to life, liberty, and the pursuit of happiness, help me to want those things to the degree that you want them for me. Help me to interact with others completely free of demanding or expecting them to treat me the way I want to be treated. And help me to put away all the bitterness and wrath my spirit of entitlement has fostered in me.

In the precious and holy name of Your Son, Jesus Christ. Amen.

THE VICTORY LIES IN THE EFFORT, NOT THE RESULT

It is not the critic who counts, nor the man who points out how the strong man stumbled or where the doer of deeds could have done them better. The credit belongs to the man who is actually in the arena; whose face is marred by dust and sweat and blood.

THEODORE ROOSEVELT

Not that I have already obtained all this, or have already arrived at my goal, but I press on to take hold of that for which Christ Jesus took hold of me.

PHILIPPIANS 3:12

Another way the enemy tries to attack us is by tempting us to tie our victory, accomplishment, and joy to whether our efforts have led to the outcomes we want. Given we can't control outcomes, this mindset leads to us feeling we've wasted our time in pursuing goals when our efforts were unsuccessful. A crucial aspect of renewing our minds is for us to shift our sense of victory and accomplishment to the *effort* we put into a pursuing a goal, not in the *achievement* of it. We need to overcome the idea that great effort always leads to great results . . . and that when it doesn't, we wasted our time. Had Wile E. Coyote thought that way, there would have only been one episode of *The Road Runner Show*, and not the almost fifty that were produced.

If effort is the key factor on which we need to focus—not the outcome—it means *perseverance* is absolutely crucial in life. If we persevere in trying to accomplish a reasonable goal, then we can claim victory whether or not we were successful in reaching that goal. With this in mind, let's first assess how we are doing when it comes to persevering in life, and then we will go into setting goals and mapping out a plan for how to achieve them.

Assessing Your PERSEVERANCE

In *The Lies We Believe*, I turned *perseverance* into an acronym that you can use to help you better understand what the word means. Let me remind you what each letter represents so that when you do the self-assessment, you will know how to respond to each statement.

P   Patience: exhibiting a quiet steadiness that doesn't look for quick success

E   Endurance: bearing pain along the way and lasting in the face of it

R   Resiliency: bouncing right back up after a setback and trying again

S   Sacrifice: surrendering your resources in the pursuit of a goal

E   Effort: exerting sufficient energy to accomplish something

V   Vision: having a clear sense of what you are trying to achieve

E   Experience: allowing your efforts and the outcome to shape your next effort

R   Relationships: including others to secure their support and encouragement

A   Attitude: bringing an attitude of optimism and confidence to your efforts

N   Necessity: doing whatever it properly takes to achieve your goal

C   Courage: bypassing your fear and doing the right thing even if it costs you

E   Enthusiasm: having positive emotional energy in the midst of your pursuits

Now, from a positive perspective, let's assess areas of your life where you have demonstrated these qualities of perseverance.

Patience: Goals I Was Patient About Achieving

_____

_____

_____

_____

_____

Endurance: Healthy Ways I Endured Setbacks in Pursuing Goals

_____

_____

_____

_____

_____

Resiliency: Ways I Bounced Back After Setbacks

_____

_____

_____

_____

_____

Sacrifice: Ways I Sacrificed to Achieve Goals

_____

_____

_____

_____

_____

Effort: Ways I Exerted the Right Amount of Effort to Achieve Goals

_____

_____

_____

_____

_____

Vision: Goals I Had a Clear Vision for How to Achieve

_____

_____

_____

_____

_____

Experience: Ways I Relied on My Experience in Achieving Goals

_____

_____

_____

_____

_____

Relationships: People I Turned to for Support in Achieving Goals

_____

_____

_____

_____

_____

Attitude: Goals in Which I Portrayed a Confident and Optimistic Attitude

_____

_____

_____

_____

_____

Necessity: Ways I Was Willing to Do What Was Necessary to Achieve Goals

_____

_____

_____

_____

_____

Courage: Ways I Was Willing to Press Through My Fears to Achieve Goals

_____

_____

_____

_____

_____

_____

Enthusiasm: Ways I Brought Energy and Enthusiasm to Achieving Goals

_____

_____

_____

_____

_____

_____

The purpose of this exercise was to help you remember the times when you brought perseverance into pursuing your goals. It is important to remember that with God's help, you can persevere and achieve the plans He has for you on earth. Don't lose sight of the fact that because of God's empowerment, you have what it takes to achieve realistic goals in life.

Run the Play

Think about three goals you have. The first should be a *major* life goal, such as getting an advanced degree, becoming a manager at work, or owning your own business. The second should be a *moderate* life goal, such as getting in better shape, learning a new skill, or developing a new hobby. The third should be a *minor* life goal, such as being more punctual, keeping your house clean, or calling a loved one more often.

Choose Your Goal

Choose one goal in each of these areas that you would like to achieve in the months and years to come. As you do this, make sure you are not choosing too lofty of a goal in any category—make sure it is doable, given your talents and abilities. For example, in the major life goal category, don't put down "become a Nobel laureate in economics" if you can't even balance your checkbook, or "become an Olympic athlete" if you can't walk and chew gum at the same time. Keep it real when choosing your goals. Don't defeat yourself before you even get started by aspiring to achieve something that isn't possible for you.

Major Goal I Want to Achieve

_____

_____

_____

_____

Moderate Goal I Want to Achieve

_____

_____

_____

_____

Minor Goal I Want to Achieve

_____

_____

_____

_____

Develop a Plan

John L. Beckley, an author and businessman, once said, "Most people don't plan to fail, they fail to plan." Obviously, you can't pursue a goal without making a realistic plan for how to accomplish it. Again, this plan should be grounded in reality. For example, if you want to get in better shape but your plan is to work out five hours a day every week, that's not going to happen. Make your goals *and* your plans for achieving them as practical and realistic as you can. Also, consider running your plan by a trusted friend, accountability partner, or counselor who can give you feedback as to how realistic and practical you are being.

Ways I Can Achieve My Major Goal

_____

_____

_____

_____

Ways I Can Achieve My Moderate Goal

_____

_____

_____

_____

Ways I Can Achieve My Minor Goal

_____

_____

_____

_____

Persevere in the Plan

Once you've developed your plans, **PERSEVERANCE** will be the key for achieving your goals and gaining more confidence that life can turn out well. Too many people today develop a defeatist attitude when it comes to achieving important goals. For this reason, you need to be **P**atient, **E**ndure setbacks, **R**esiliently bounce back from defeats, **S**acrificially put time/energy/talent into what you are doing, exert **E**ffort in what you are doing, stay focused on the **V**ision, allow **E**xperience to help you improve, rely on your **R**elationships, have the right **A**ttitude, do what is **N**ecessary to achieve the goal, **C**ourageously move through your fears, and stay **E**nthusiastic about just how good your future can be with God's help and support along the way.

If you can believe victory is found in the *effort* and not the *results*, you will experience so much more than you ever hoped for or imagined in life. God doesn't look at the results as much as He looks at your heart and whether you gave an endeavor your best effort. If your heart is in the right place and your effort is vigorous enough, He is going to say, "Well done, good and faithful servant," and put what you did in the win column.

Count on it.

Key Memory and Meditation Verses

Let us not become weary in doing good, for at the proper time we will reap a harvest if we do not give up (Galatians 6:9).

Not that I have already obtained all this, or have already arrived at my goal, but I press on to take hold of that for which Christ Jesus took hold of me (Philippians 3:12).

Being strengthened with all power according to his glorious might so that you may have great endurance and patience (Colossians 1:11).

You need to persevere so that when you have done the will of God, you will receive what he has promised (Hebrews 10:36).

And let us run with perseverance the race marked out for us (Hebrews 12:1).

Blessed is the one who perseveres under trial because, having stood the test, that person will receive the crown of life that the Lord has promised to those who love him (James 1:12).

Contemplative Prayer
(to be read slowly, meditatively, and repeatedly)

Heavenly Father,

I find myself getting easily discouraged at times. I often want to throw in the towel and give up on pursuing the goals and visions You have laid out for me. I know the enemy wants me to grow weary in doing what is right and quit pressing on to the mark of becoming more like Your Son.

Please, Father, help me to get better at each of the aspects of perseverance. Help me to be more patient as I pursue my goals, endure the pain along the way, bounce back when I'm knocked down, surrender my resources when needed, exert sufficient energy, have a clear sense of what I am trying to achieve, allow my progress to shape my future efforts, rely on the support and encouragement of others, bring an attitude of optimism and confidence to my endeavors, do whatever is necessary within Your moral constraints to achieve my goals, be courageous in the face of threatening challenges, and have positive emotional energy in the midst of my pursuits. Allow me to persevere in the face of difficult challenges so that with Your help and good will, I can accomplish what You have laid out before me in life.

In the precious and holy name of Your Son, Jesus Christ. Amen.

YOU ARE GOING TO DIE

*Pale death with impartial tread beats at the poor
man's cottage door and at the palaces of king.*

HORACE

*Who can live and not see death, or who can
escape the power of the grave?*

PSALM 89:48

The funeral bell is going to toll for each of us one day. Many of us *intellectually* assent to the fact that death is around the corner, but we tend to stiff-arm this truth and not allow it to motivate us to live more fully and passionately. We really do only go around once in life, and we need to grab for all the healthy spiritual, psychological, and relational gusto available to us. Given the reality that "people are destined to die once" (Hebrews 9:27), the million-dollar question as theologian Francis Schaeffer posed it is, "How should we then live?" Let's drill into that question by first dealing with the prospects of our death and doing some self-assessment.

The Stages of Grief

In *The Lies We Believe*, I explained how Swiss psychiatrist Elisabeth Kübler-Ross created a theory of grief that suggested people move through five stages when facing death: (1) denial, (2) anger, (3) bargaining, (4) depression, and (5) acceptance.[3] In the spaces below, write down how you are doing in each stage of this model (commonly known by the acronym DABDA). Be as honest as you can about whether you are progressing through these stages, are stuck in one of them, or might have jumped around from one stage to another.

Denial: Ways I Have Avoided the Reality That I'm Going to Die

_____

_____

_____

_____

_____

_____

Anger: Ways I Have Felt Angry About the Fact I Am Going to Die

_____

_____

_____

_____

_____

_____

Bargaining: Ways I Have Bargained with God About My Death

_____

_____

_____

_____

_____

_____

<u>D</u>epression: Ways I Have Felt Sad About the Fact I Am Going to Die

_____

_____

_____

_____

_____

_____

<u>A</u>cceptance: Ways I Have Accepted the Reality of My Death

_____

_____

_____

_____

_____

_____

Step back from what you wrote down. What is your overall impression of how you have dealt with the reality that "people are destined to die . . . and after that to face judgment" (Hebrews 9:27)? How has your approach to death positively or negatively impacted your life?

_____

_____

_____

_____

Live Like You're Going to Die

Psychiatrist Irvin Yalom once conducted research with people who had terminal cancer to determine how it impacted their lives. He discovered that once they accepted the fact their lives were drawing to an end, it resulted in (1) a rearrangement of their priorities; (2) a sense of liberation (they could choose to not do the things they did not wish to do); (3) an enhanced sense of living in the present; (4) an appreciation of the elemental facts of life (changing seasons, warmth of the sun, a fresh breeze); (5) a deeper communication with loved ones; and (6) fewer fears, less concern about rejection, and greater willingness to take risks.[4]

In the following section, use these findings to consider how you would live your life differently if you knew you were going to die *five years* from this very moment. In the spaces provided below, write down how you would address each of these areas *as you continue to keep fulfilling your roles in life* (job, spouse, parent, friend, follower of Christ). Make sure everything you write down is consistent with following through on the commitments you made to yourself, to others, and to God in regard to the roles you took on in life.

How It Would Help Me Rearrange My Priorities

_____

_____

_____

_____

_____

_____

How It Would Help Me Trivialize the Trivial

_____

_____

_____

_____

_____

_____

How It Would Help Me Stop Doing Unimportant Things

_____

_____

_____

_____

_____

_____

**How It Would Help Me Live in the Present
and Do "Bucket List" Items**

_____
_____
_____
_____
_____
_____

How It Would Help Me Appreciate the Elemental Aspects of Life

_____
_____
_____
_____
_____
_____

How It Would Help Me Communicate More Deeply with Loved Ones

_____
_____
_____
_____
_____
_____

How It Would Help Me Reconcile with Others (If Possible)

_____
_____
_____
_____
_____
_____

How It Would Help Me to Interact *More* with These People (and Why)

_____

_____

_____

_____

_____

How It Would Help Me to Interact *Less* with These People (and Why)

_____

_____

_____

_____

_____

How It Would Help Me to Have Fewer Interpersonal Fears

_____

_____

_____

_____

_____

How It Would Help Me to Take Greater Risks

_____

_____

_____

_____

_____

How It Would Deepen My Spiritual Life

_____
_____
_____
_____
_____
_____

Take a deep breath—you've done a lot of good work here in thinking about your life in a more constructive and meaningful way. After you've collected yourself, go back through each of the categories listed above, and then choose *one* item you are going to implement in how you are going to live for the next five years. Write it out in the space below.

_____
_____
_____
_____
_____
_____

I strongly encourage you to follow through on implementing each of these items so your life will be more abundant. Like it or not, we only go around once in life. Once the funeral bell tolls, everything goes back in the box called "life" and is permanently sealed. So let's live this life with as much spiritual, psychological, and relational gusto as we can.

Key Memory and Meditation Verses

Show me, LORD, my life's end and the number of my days; let me know how fleeting my life is (Psalm 39:4).

The life of mortals is like grass, they flourish like a flower of the field; the wind blows over it and it is gone, and its place remembers it no more (Psalm 103:15–16).

The fear of the LORD leads to life; then one rests content, untouched by trouble (Proverbs 19:23).

There is a time for everything, and a season for every activity under the heavens: a time to be born and a time to die (Ecclesiastes 3:1–2).

In this way they will lay up treasure for themselves as a firm foundation for the coming age, so that they may take hold of the life that is truly life (1 Timothy 6:19).

Just as people are destined to die once, and after that to face judgment, so Christ was sacrificed once to take away the sins of many (Hebrews 9:27–28).

Contemplative Prayer
(to be read slowly, meditatively, and repeatedly)

Heavenly Father,

You have made it clear I only get one life and after that I die, I will either go to a place of eternal rest with You or eternal torment apart from You. I have played into being in denial about death, angry about the reality of it, and have even bargained with You at times about when and how my death is going to happen. Father, I ask You to help me break out of my feelings of denial about the reality of my death, to not be angry about it, and to not foolishly try to bargain with you about it. I ask for Your help to live life more fully in light of the fact that my days are numbered and there is no guarantee I am even going to have tomorrow.

Father, please help me to rearrange my priorities, trivialize the trivial, stop doing things that are unimportant, appreciate the elemental aspects of life, communicate on a deeper level with loved ones, reconcile where I can with others, do bucket list items, take appropriate risks, seek people's approval less, interact with some people more and less with others, and deepen my spiritual life. I only have this one life, so help me to live it fully and in a way that honors and glorifies You.

In the precious and holy name of Your Son, Jesus Christ. Amen.

PART FOUR

The Truth
Will Set
You Free

WHAT WOULD JESUS THINK?

*It is important that we know who Christ is,
especially the chief characteristic that is the root
and essence of His character as our Redeemer.
There can be but one answer: it is His humility.*

ANDREW MURRAY

*"Come to me, all you who are weary and burdened,
and I will give you rest. Take my yoke upon you
and learn from me, for I am gentle and humble
in heart, and you will find rest for your souls."*

MATTHEW 11:28–29

The main quality of the mind of Christ was humility. All the thoughts that went through His mind were not only perfectly accurate but also perfectly free of arrogance or pride. In light of this fact, to develop the mind of Christ, we need to ask God to continually help us take arrogant thoughts captive, cast them down, and filter the things that happen to us through the humble and unpretentious thoughts that constantly went through the mind of Christ. To move in that direction, I want you to complete the following self-assessment questionnaire and be as honest as you can about how humble your thoughts are as you go into the world each day.

Assessing Your Beliefs

Complete the self-assessment inventory using the scale below. As I have said a hundred times before, be honest about what you *actually think* and avoid responding in terms of how you *should think*. You don't want to fall into what assessment professionals call "faking good" by trying to make yourself look better than you are. At the same time, you don't want to fall into "faking bad" by making yourself look worse than you are. As you go through this self-assessment try to avoid using the neutral response (*4*) in your answers as much as you can.

1	2	3	4	5	6	7
Strongly Disagree			Neutral			Strongly Agree

_____ 1. I believe every human being is made in the image of God and possesses inherent worth.

_____ 2. I believe in serving and not being served.

_____ 3. I believe in not returning wrong for wrong when people mistreat me.

_____ 4. I believe in giving people more than what they asked for in an effort to be at peace with them.

_____ 5. I believe in honest self-examination and taking the "plank" out of my own eye.

_____ 6. I believe it is human to make mistakes and wrong to shame myself and others when we prove how human we are.

_____ 7. I believe it is wrong to try to control others and that my focus needs to be on exercising *self-control* and *influencing* others.

_____ 8. I am not entitled to love, respect, and fairness while I'm here.

_____ 9. I believe my fallen nature is bent toward sin in the forms of selfishness, laziness, and immaturity.

_____ 10. I believe it is appropriate to feel sad, hurt, and angry in the face of the painful things that happen to us in life.

_____ 11. I believe it is better to face difficult problems in life than to run from them.

_____ 12. I believe in submitting to authority as long as people do not ask me to violate my moral and ethical integrity before a holy God.

_____ 13. I believe everyone has to experience painful suffering in order to grow.

_____ 14. I believe in pleasing God and not humankind.

_____ 15. I believe the way people treat me is about them and their issues.

_____ 16. I believe how I respond to mistreatment is about me and not the person who mistreated me.

_____ 17. I believe good intentions are not enough and that you have to back them up with action.

_____ 18. I believe that victory is in the effort and not the outcome.

_____ 19. I believe physical death awaits me and that I'm not going to get another chance at life.

_____ 20. I believe *agape* love never fails, whether or not people receive it or return it.

From my perspective, these are all correct ways of thinking and represent the mindset of Christ while He was here. Look back through your answers and circle any statement you gave a *1, 2,* or *3*, as these responses indicate you are not looking at life in the healthy and humble way that Christ did. As with the other self-assessments, I am not trying to rub your nose in how faulty your views are—I am simply trying to heighten your awareness of the enemy's efforts to get you to think in ways that are un-Christlike and causing damage to your life.

Working on the Mind of Christ

The apostle Paul writes that we are to "have the same mindset as Christ Jesus" (Philippians 2:5), which means having the same mindset of humility that Christ possessed. With this in mind, in the spaces provided below I want you to write down how well your attitude aligns with the attitude Jesus had during His time on earth. Again, don't beat yourself up, but remember that Jesus was God in human form and yet was humble in how He viewed life—while we are fallen image-bearers who fall into many prideful and arrogant thoughts. Be completely honest when it comes to comparing your attitude to the attitude Jesus had in His interactions with people.

Jesus Believed Every Human Was Fearfully and Wonderfully Made

"Are not two sparrows sold for a penny? Yet not one of them will fall to the ground outside your Father's care. . . . You are worth more than many sparrows" (Matthew 10:29, 31).

_____
_____
_____
_____

Jesus Believed in Serving, Not Being Served

"For even the Son of Man did not come to be served, but to serve" (Mark 10:45).

_____
_____
_____
_____

Jesus Believed in Turning the Other Cheek

"Do not resist an evil person. If anyone slaps you on the right cheek, turn to them the other cheek also" (Matthew 5:39).

_____
_____
_____
_____

Jesus Believed in Giving People More Than They Deserved

"If someone takes your coat, do not withhold your shirt from them" (Luke 6:29).

_____
_____
_____
_____

Jesus Believed in Honest Self-Examination

"Why do you look at the speck of sawdust in your brother's eye and pay no attention to the plank in your own eye?" (Matthew 7:3).

_____

_____

_____

_____

Jesus Believed It Was Wrong to Condemn People for Making Mistakes

"Neither do I condemn you. . . . "Go now and leave your life of sin" (John 8:11).

_____

_____

_____

_____

Jesus Believed It Was Wrong to Control Others

Jesus answered, "If you want to be perfect, go, sell your possessions. . . . Then come, follow me." When the young man heard this, he went away sad, because he had great wealth (Matthew 19:21–22).

_____

_____

_____

_____

Jesus Did Not Believe He Was Entitled to Love, Respect, or Fairness

He then began to teach them that the Son of Man must suffer many things and be rejected by the elders, the chief priests and the teachers of the law (Mark 8:31).

_____

_____

_____

_____

Jesus Felt Hurt, Angry, and Sad About Bad Things That Happen in Life

When Jesus saw [Mary] weeping, and the Jews who had come along with her also weeping, he was deeply moved in spirit and troubled (John 11:33).

_____

_____

_____

_____

Jesus Believed It Was Better to Face Problems Than Avoid Them

[Jesus] said to his disciples, "Let us go back to Judea." "But Rabbi," they said, "a short while ago the Jews there tried to stone you, and yet you are going back?" (John 11:7–8).

_____

_____

_____

_____

Jesus Believed in Properly Submitting to Authority

Jesus said to them, "Give back to Caesar what is Caesar's and to God what is God's" (Mark 12:17).

_____

_____

_____

_____

Jesus Believed Everyone Had to Undergo the Growth Process . . . Even Himself

Jesus grew in wisdom and stature, and in favor with God and man (Luke 2:52).

_____

_____

_____

_____

Jesus Believed in Pleasing God the Father, Not People
"But seek first [God's] kingdom and his righteousness" (Matthew 6:33).

_____

_____

_____

_____

_____

Jesus Believed How People Treated Him Was About Them
Jesus said, "Father, forgive them, for they do not know what they are doing" (Luke 23:34).

_____

_____

_____

_____

_____

Jesus Believed Good Intentions Were Never Enough
Jesus said to him, "Today salvation has come to this house. . . . For the Son of Man came to seek and to save the lost" (Luke 19:9–10).

_____

_____

_____

_____

_____

Jesus Believed the Victory Is in the Effort, Not the Outcome
Jesus said to them, "My Father is always at his work to this very day, and I too am working" (John 5:17).

_____

_____

_____

_____

_____

Jesus Believed Physical Death Awaited Everyone . . . Even Himself

"The Son of Man . . .will be delivered over to the Gentiles. They will mock him, insult him and spit on him; they will flog him and kill him" (Luke 18:31–33).

_____

_____

_____

_____

Jesus Believed That Real Love (*Agape*) Never Fails

Jesus replied: "'Love the Lord your God with all your heart and with all your soul and with all your mind.' This is the first and greatest commandment" (Matthew 22:37–38).

_____

_____

_____

_____

_____

We live in a day and age where we are told to "awaken the giant within," "look out for number one," "climb the ladder of success," and "be the king/queen of the hill." How has that worked for us? All it seems to have done is puff up people's pride and lead many of them to use others as objects in their quest for personal glory. Jesus believed in awakening the spirit inside of others, looking out for them, descending the ladder of success (even to death on a cross), and viewing the lowest as being the greatest in God's kingdom. Jesus' humility is dumbfounding in light of the fact He was the co-creator of the universe and everything was under His authority. We would do well to pursue the same attitude He had—an attitude of humility.

Key Memory and Meditation Verses

Memorize three verses from the list above that spoke the most powerfully to you as it relates to having the mindset of Christ. Spend some time this week meditating specifically on those verses so God can help you get the most meaning and significance from them as you can.

Contemplative Prayer
(to be read slowly, meditatively, and repeatedly)

Heavenly Father,

Help me to view reality the way Your Son did during His time on earth. Develop in me an attitude of humility where I value others above myself, look to their interests, and treat them with honor and dignity. Help me not to envy others but to be happy for them when good things come their way. Enable me to patiently and graciously bear with the flaws and defects of others and never think that I am better than them. Help me not to boast in myself or my accomplishments but to boast in you for equipping me to do your will.

Father, I also ask that You would help me to never look down on anyone and to hold all people in high esteem as Your image-bearers. I know that pride goes before a fall, and I pray that You will help me to avoid any whiff of arrogance or haughtiness in my interactions with others. Even though You are God, You are humble—something that is truly hard to grasp. Please help me—as a finite and fallen human being—to clothe myself in humility each and every day.

In the precious and holy name of Your Son, Jesus Christ. Amen.

THE HUMILITY OF CHRIST IN INTERACTING WITH PEOPLE

I know men and I tell you that Jesus Christ is no mere man.
Between him and every other person in the world there is no
possible term of comparison. . . . Jesus Christ founded his empire
upon love; and at this hour millions of men would die for him.

NAPOLEON

A new command I give you: Love one another. As I have
loved you, so you must love one another. By this everyone
will know you are my disciples, if you love one another.

JOHN 13:34–35

The bottom line in our relationship with Christ is whether we are treating people in a loving manner. The apostle Paul made this clear when he wrote, "If I speak in the tongues of men or of angels, but do not have love, I am only a resounding gong or a clanging cymbal. If I have the gift of prophecy and can fathom all mysteries and all knowledge, and if I have faith that can move mountains, but do not have love, I am nothing. If I give all I possess to the poor and give over my body to hardship that I may boast, but do not have love, I gain nothing" (1 Corinthians 13:1–3). The defining characteristic of a Christian is our love for others (see John 13:35).

In the previous lesson, we explored how the attitude of Christ was one of humility. It was this attitude that enabled Him to be loving toward everyone He encountered. If we do not have humility as we go through life, we will not be able to truly love others. In light of this fact, in this lesson I want you to focus on *three people* to whom you need to humble yourself toward and extend more love in their direction.

Three People I Am Going to Love More Deeply

All of us have people in our lives whom we need to love in a deeper and richer way. In this section, I want you to ask God to bring three of these people to mind. Note that if you are estranged from someone right now, exclude that person from the list if he or she has a hardened heart toward you and is not willing to repair the relationship. When Christ told Judas, "What you are about to do, do quickly" (John 13:27), He was letting Judas know their relationship was irreparably broken and there would be no further effort to repair it. So, as you ask God to help you choose three people to *interactively* love more fully, head in the direction of those who are healthy and humble enough to join you in the effort to heal things and restore the relationship to a more loving place.

Person #1: _____

The prideful and arrogant attitudes I have had toward this person that has gotten in the way of me loving them more fully:

_____

_____

The humble attitude I need to have toward this person:

_____

_____

Specific ways I can love this person with all my heart, mind, soul, and strength:

_____

_____

_____

_____

How, when, and where I am going to put this into action:

_____

_____

_____

_____

Person #2: _____

The prideful and arrogant attitudes I have had toward this person that has gotten in the way of me loving them more fully:

_____

_____

The humble attitude I need to have toward this person:

_____

_____

Specific ways I can love this person with all my heart, mind, soul, and strength:

_____

_____

_____

_____

How, when, and where I am going to put this into action:

_____

_____

_____

_____

Person #3: _____

The prideful and arrogant attitudes I have had toward this person that has gotten in the way of me loving them more fully:

_____

_____

The humble attitude I need to have toward this person:

_____

_____

Specific ways I can love this person with all my heart, mind, soul, and strength:

_____

_____

_____

_____

How, when, and where I am going to put this into action:

_____

_____

_____

_____

The bottom line is to not merely *tell* people we love them but to *show* them we love them. When Jesus was on earth, He didn't just tell people He loved them—He showed them by healing them, feeding them, listening to them, teaching them the truth, affirming them, and challenging them when it was appropriate. The greatest expression of Christ's love through action was His death on the cross as a payment for our sins. As Paul wrote, "God demonstrates His own love for us in this: While we were still sinners, Christ died for us" (Romans 5:8).

We all grow up hearing a lot of platitudes thrown our way. One of the most important is this: *talk is cheap*. So ask God on a daily basis to help you quit merely *talking* about how you love the people in your life and start actually *showing* them that you love them through your actions. Anything short of this isn't love.

Key Memory and Meditation Verses

"You have heard that it was said, 'Love your neighbor and hate your enemy.' But I tell you, love your enemies and pray for those who persecute you" (Matthew 5:43).

Be devoted to one another in love. Honor one another above yourselves (Romans 12:10).

Follow God's example, therefore, as dearly loved children and walk in the way of love, just as Christ loved us and gave himself up for us as a fragrant offering and sacrifice to God (Ephesians 5:1–2).

And let us consider how we may spur one another on toward love and good deeds (Hebrews 10:24).

Above all, love each other deeply, because love covers over a multitude of sins (1 Peter 4:8).

This is how we know what love is: Jesus Christ laid down his life for us. And we ought to lay down our lives for our brothers and sisters (1 John 3:16).

Contemplative Prayer
(to be read slowly, meditatively, and repeatedly)

Heavenly Father,

You love the people in the world so much that You sent Your only Son to die for our sins. There is no greater love than that. If I claim to love You but don't love my neighbor, I make myself a liar. You ask that those who claim to be followers of Christ devote themselves to loving others, and I ask for Your help to obey You in this endeavor. Left to my own human efforts, I know I would fail at loving others. You being love is the only hope I have for loving others well. I pray that You would make my love increase for others—that it would overflow toward my neighbor because Your love in me overflows toward Your creation.

Help me, Father, not to shrink back from loving others in a way that is sacrificial and costly, especially when it comes to those who have sought to do me harm.

Please empower me to go through each day looking for opportunities to love others deeply and well and with no strings attached. Help me to be a conduit of Your love to a world that is in such desperate need of it. Enable me to have the attitude of Christ toward others in that He came to serve and not to be served. Please, God, help me to avoid rationalizing or justifying those times when I withhold love just because someone withheld it from me.

In the precious and holy name of Your Son, Jesus Christ. Amen.

STAYING THE COURSE IN RENEWING YOUR MIND

The transformation of our thought life by taking on the mind of Christ—his ideas, images, information, and patterns of thinking—opens the way to deliverance of every dimension of the human self from the oppressive powers of darkness.

DALLAS WILLARD

Let us run with perseverance the race marked out for us, fixing our eyes on Jesus, the pioneer and perfecter of faith. For the joy set before him he endured the cross, scorning its shame, and sat down at the right hand of the throne of God.

HEBREWS 12:1–2

The focus of this workbook has been on helping you pursue what is "true . . . noble . . . right . . . pure . . . lovely . . . admirable" (Philippians 4:8), not on what is false, ignoble, wrong, impure, unlovely, and unworthy. By focusing on what is true, I hope that you have strengthened those thoughts in your mind while simultaneously weakening the lies you have believed. Nevertheless, "the lies we believe" are still there—and they still want to dictate how you view reality. With this in mind, in this final lesson I want you to take some time to think about what lies are still prevalent in your mind in terms of how you view yourself, others, life, and God.

The Lies That Just Don't Seem to Go Away

In spite of our best efforts, we can still find ourselves thinking in false and unbiblical ways. When this happens, it is a reflection of how deep-seated some of the lies we believe have become and how much we have rehearsed them over and over again in our minds. The enemy wants us to be discouraged about overcoming these lies—but with God's help, and our commitment, we can have the victory. Let's take a minute to go back through each of the lessons on the lies we believe and see which ones may still be holding us in bondage.

The Deadliest Lie I Still Believe About Myself

In lesson 4, "The Lies We Believe About Ourselves," we explored a number of lies we often struggle with when it comes to how we view ourselves. Let me remind you what they were:

- I'm worthless.
- I'm unworthy of love.
- When there is a rupture in a relationship, it is always my fault.
- It isn't okay to be a human being and make mistakes.
- My worth is determined by how I perform.
- I must have everyone's love and approval.
- It is easier to avoid my problems than to face them.
- My unhappiness is externally caused.

Which of these lies do you still believe fairly strongly?

_____

What have you learned during this study that counters this lie?

_____
_____
_____
_____
_____

What is leading you to still believe this particular lie? What do you think you need to do to ratchet up your efforts to replace it with the truth?

_____

_____

_____

_____

_____

What single verse or passage of Scripture have you found to combat this lie? Write the verse below in your own words, and then try to find as many ways as possible to restate what that verse or passage is saying to you. Don't hold back in giving full expression to what you think the Word of God is telling you when it comes to the importance of this truth to set you free.

_____

_____

_____

_____

_____

_____

The Deadliest Lie I Still Believe About Others

Not only do we tend to fail to see ourselves the way God wants us to see ourselves, but we also fail to see other people clearly as well. In lesson 5, "The Lies We Believe About Others," we explored some of these false views that we often carry about other people. Here is a reminder of the lies we covered in that lesson:

- People can meet all my emotional needs.
- Others should accept me just the way I am.
- To get along, everyone needs to think, feel, and act the same way.
- Others are more messed up than me.
- People who hurt me have to earn my forgiveness.

Which of these lies do you still believe fairly strongly?

_____

What have you learned during this study to counter this lie?

_____

_____

_____

_____

_____

What is leading you to still believe this particular lie? What do you think you need to do to ratchet up your efforts to replace it with the truth?

_____

_____

_____

_____

_____

What single verse or passage of Scripture have you found to combat this lie? Write the verse below in your own words, and then try to find as many ways as possible to restate what that verse or passage is saying to you. Don't hold back in giving full expression to what you think the Word of God is telling you when it comes to the importance of this truth to set you free.

_____

_____

_____

_____

_____

_____

The Deadliest Lie I Still Believe About Life

In lesson 6, "The Lies We Believe About Life," we explored the faulty beliefs we carry around each day as we pursue "the good life." We are told that we have the right to life, liberty, and the pursuit of happiness, but if we aren't careful, we can interpret that to mean life *owes* us these things (or we mis-define what having these things would look like). While there are numerous lies we can fall into about life, we explored six of what may be the deadliest:

- You can have it all.
- You shouldn't wait for what you want.
- You can do anything you set your mind to.
- Being happy is the most important thing in life.
- Life should be easy and fair.
- People are basically good.

Which of these lies do you still believe fairly strongly?

_____

What have you learned during this study to counter this lie?

_____
_____
_____
_____

What is leading you to still believe this particular lie? What do you think you need to do to ratchet up your efforts to replace it with the truth?

_____
_____
_____
_____
_____

What single verse or passage of Scripture have you found to combat this lie? Write the verse below in your own words, and then try to find as many ways as possible to restate what that verse or passage is saying to you. Don't hold back in giving full expression to what you think the Word of God is telling you when it comes to the importance of this truth to set you free.

_____
_____
_____
_____

The Deadliest Lie I Still Believe About God

In lesson 7, "The Lies We Believe About God," we explored the idea that the way we view God is the most important thing about ourselves and will significantly impact how we go through life. While there are numerous lies the enemy tries to convince us to accept about God, we explored several of the most common ones:

- God's love must be earned.
- God is mean and vindictive.
- God ignores our disobedience.
- God gives us whatever we want.
- God has lost control of everything.

Which of these lies do you still believe fairly strongly?

_____

What have you learned during this study to counter this lie?

_____

_____

_____

_____

_____

What is leading you to still believe this particular lie? What do you think you need to do to ratchet up your efforts to replace it with the truth?

_____

_____

_____

_____

_____

_____

What single verse or passage of Scripture have you found to counter this lie? Write the verse below in your own words, and then try to find as many ways as possible to restate what that verse or passage is saying to you. Don't hold back in giving full expression to what you think the Word of God is telling you when it comes to the importance of this truth to set you free.

_____

_____

_____

_____

The Deadliest Lie I Still Believe About
Myself as a Man (or About Men)

In lesson 8, "The Lies Men Believe," we explored several unbiblical ways of thinking into which men may be prone to fall. Here is the list of lies we covered:

- I don't have what it takes to be a man.
- It's not okay to feel sad, scared, or hurt.
- My good intentions ought to satisfy everyone.
- Sex is about my pleasure and enjoyment.
- I can do it by myself.

Which of these lies do you still believe fairly strongly?

_____

What have you learned during this study to counter this lie?

_____

_____

_____

_____

What is leading you to still believe this particular lie? What do you think you need to do to ratchet up your efforts to replace it with the truth?

_____

_____

_____

_____

What single verse or passage of Scripture have you found to combat this lie? Write the verse below in your own words, and then try to find as many ways as possible to restate what that verse or passage is saying to you. Don't hold back in giving full expression to what you think the Word of God is telling you when it comes to the importance of this truth to set you free.

_____

_____

_____

_____

_____

_____

The Deadliest Lie I Still Believe About Myself as a Woman (or About Women)

In lesson 9, "The Lies Women Believe," we explored several different lies that women may be prone to believe. Here is the list of lies we covered:

- My main job in life is to make everyone happy.
- It's not okay to speak my mind.
- I'm facing my flaws.
- I'm not worthy of being loved for who I am.
- Outer beauty is more important than inner beauty.

Which of these lies do you still believe fairly strongly?

_____

What have you learned during this study to counter this lie?

_____

_____

_____

_____

_____

_____

What is leading you to still believe this particular lie? How might you work alongside God to replace it with the truth?

_____

_____

_____

_____

_____

What single verse or passage of Scripture have you found to combat this lie? Write the verse below in your own words, and then try to find as many ways as possible to restate what that verse or passage is saying to you. Don't hold back in giving full expression to what you think the Word of God is telling you when it comes to the importance of this truth to set you free.

_____

_____

_____

_____

_____

_____

Some of these faulty ways of thinking about ourselves, others, and God are more deeply embedded in how we view reality than others. These are "core" beliefs that can lead to a great deal of emotional and behavioral dysregulation in our lives. To put it differently, it is hard to overcome a way of thinking we have been rehearsing in our minds ever since we were young. As Paul wrote, "When I was a child, I talked like a child, I thought like a child, I reasoned like a child" (1 Corinthians 13:11). However, we should not be discouraged, because as Paul concluded in that verse, we can choose as adults to "put the ways of childhood" behind us.

Even if you have thought in an unbiblical way for decades, God, through the Holy Spirit, can and will continue to help you take your thoughts captive, cast down toxic mental strongholds, and grow to have core beliefs about reality that are true, noble, right, pure, lovely, and admirable. In this way, instead of reacting to life in unhealthy ways, we can learn to react in ways that reflect how Christ responded to things that were disturbing and painful to Him.

The Truths I Believe More Deeply

Hopefully, given that you have been working for a while now on the renewal of your mind, there are certain truths you believe more deeply than when you first began this journey. Take a few minutes to write down which three truths from this study are helping you to cope with life in a healthier and more Christlike manner. Also write down what has helped you to believe that truth in your heart on a deeper level.

Truth #1 I Believe More Deeply (and Why):

_____

_____

_____

_____

_____

_____

_____

Truth #2 I Believe More Deeply (and Why):

_____

_____

_____

_____

_____

_____

_____

Truth #3 I Believe More Deeply (and Why):

_____

_____

_____

_____

_____

_____

Keep Thinking on What Is True, Right, and Admirable

The dedication at the beginning of *The Lies We Believe* reads, "To truth seekers everywhere." As you conclude this study, I want you to know that *you* are the one to whom this is addressed. The fact that you have read *The Lies We Believe* and completed the workbook marks you as a truth seeker. People who start studies like this often stop after completing only one or two lessons. These are people to whom the apostle Paul referred when he said:

> For the time will come when the people will not put up with sound doctrine. Instead, to suit their own desires, they gather around them a great number of teachers to say what their itching ears want to hear (2 Timothy 4:3).

In reading the book and completing this workbook, you have courageously worked through a number of challenging truths your "itching ears" probably didn't want to hear. But you heard these truths anyway and courageously implemented them into your life. Well done!

I encourage you now to not grow weary in your pursuit of truth and the freedom it brings. Given the effort you have put into the renewal of your mind, you are more of a threat to the enemy than ever before—and he is going to do whatever he can to discourage and defeat you. However, if you keep turning to God for His truth, He will empower your efforts. Remember, "even youths grow tired and weary, and young men stumble and fall; but those who hope in the LORD will renew their strength. They will soar on wings like eagles; they will run and not grow weary, they will walk and not be faint" (Isaiah 40:30–31).

May God continue to richly bless you in your pursuit of truth. May He empower everything you do to renew your mind with His truth so you can follow in the footsteps of Christ. And may He work through you, both inside and outside the body of Christ, to help others do the same. I will be praying for you in the months and years to come the prayer that Paul prayed for the church at Ephesus:

> I keep asking that the God of our Lord Jesus Christ, the glorious Father, may give you the Spirit of wisdom and revelation, so that you may know him better. I pray that the eyes of your heart may be enlightened in order that you may know the

hope to which he has called you, the riches of his glorious inheritance in his holy people, and his incomparably great power for us who believe (1:17–19).

May the eyes of your heart be opened . . . and may the truth set you free!

Key Memory and Meditation Verses

You will keep in perfect peace those whose minds are steadfast, because they trust in you (Isaiah 26:3).

"But the seed on good soil stands for those with a noble and good heart, who hear the word, retain it, and by persevering produce a crop" (Luke 8:15).

Not that I have already obtained all this, or have already arrived at my goal, but I press on to take hold of that for which Christ Jesus took hold of me (Philippians 3:12).

Watch your life and doctrine closely. Persevere in them, because if you do, you will save both yourself and your hearers (1 Timothy 4:16).

Let perseverance finish its work so that you may be mature and complete, not lacking anything (James 1:4).

Make every effort to add to your faith goodness; and to goodness, knowledge; and to knowledge, self-control; and to self-control, perseverance; and to perseverance, godliness; and to godliness, mutual affection; and to mutual affection, love (2 Peter 1:5–7).

Contemplative Prayer
(to be read slowly, meditatively, and repeatedly)

> *Heavenly Father,*
> *I ask today that You give me the strength to persevere in the face of the trials and setbacks that I will experience in the months and years to come. Empower my*

efforts to be transformed by the renewing of my mind and help me to not grow weary when it seems little progress is being made. Help me to continue running the race of becoming more like your Son so I can go from thinking and reasoning like a child to reasoning and thinking like a mature adult.

Father, protect me from the enemy's lies and help my heart to be receptive soil for the planting of your truth. Allow me to live in this world but not think the way it does about how to live life well. Give me the courage to run from the lies that are pleasing to hear and to believe the truth no matter how painful or upsetting it may be. Help me to be hard-working when it comes to studying and internalizing truth so that when I'm under attack, I will view things the way Christ did and respond accordingly. Thank You, God, that You are truth, that You help me through Your Holy Spirit to grow in truth, and that the truth sets me free.

In the precious and holy name of Your Son, Jesus Christ. Amen.

ENDNOTES

1. C. S. Lewis, *The Weight of Glory* (New York: HarperCollins, 1949, 2001), 26.

2. Anais Nin, *The Diary of Anais Nin, 1939–1944*, ed. Guther Stuhlmann (New York: HBJ, 1969), xiv.

3. Elisabeth Kübler-Ross, *On Death and Dying* (New York: Scribner, 1969, 1997), chaps. 3–7.

4. Dr. Irvin Yalom, *Existential Psychotherapy* (New York: Basic Books, 1980), 35.

Recommended Resources

Blackaby, Henry, and Richard Blackaby, *Experiencing God: Knowing and Doing the Will of God*, Revised Edition. Nashville, TN: B&H, 2008.

Chan, Francis, *Crazy Love*, Revised Edition. Colorado Springs, CO: David C. Cook, 2013.

Cloud, Henry, and John Townsend. *Boundaries: When to Say Yes, How to Say No to Take Control of Your Life*, updated and expanded edition. Grand Rapids, MI: Zondervan, 2017.

Foster, Richard J. Celebration of Discipline: The Path to Spiritual Growth, special 20th anniversary edition. San Francisco: HarperSanFrancisco, 1998.

Keller, Timothy. *Prayer: Experiencing Awe and Intimacy with God.* New York: Penguin Books, 2014.

———. *The Prodigal God: Recovering the Heart of the Christian Faith.* New York: Penguin Books, 2008.

a Kempis, Thomas. *The Imitation of Christ.* Mineola, NY: Dover Publications, 2003.

Knabb, Joshua. *Acceptance and Commitment Therapy for Christian Clients.* New York: Routledge, 2017.

———. *The Compassion-Based Workbook for Christian Clients.* New York: Routledge, 2019.

Lewis, C. S. *Mere Christianity*, revised and enlarged edition. New York: HarperOne, 2015.

Manning, Brennan, *The Ragamuffin Gospel: Good News for the Bedraggled, Beat Up, and Burnt Out*, anniversary edition. Colorado Springs, CO: Multnomah, 2015.

McDowell, Josh, and Sean McDowell, *More Than a Carpenter*, revised edition. Wheaton, IL: Tyndale Momentum, 2009.

Moreland, J. P. *Love Your God with All Your Mind: The Role of Reason in the Life of the Soul.* Colorado Springs, CO: NavPress, Revised, Updated Edition, 2012.

Morgan, Robert. *Reclaiming the Lost Art of Biblical Meditation: Finding True Peace in Jesus.* Nashville, TN: Thomas Nelson, 2017.

Murray, Andrew. *Humility: The Journey Toward Holiness.* Bloomington, MN: Bethany House Publishers, 2001.

Packer, J. I. *Knowing God.* Downers Grove, IL: InterVarsity Press, 1993.

Piper, John. *Think: The Life of the Mind and the Love of God.* Wheaton, IL: Crossway, 2011.

Stott, John. *Basic Christianity*, 50th anniversary edition. Downers Grove, IL: InterVarsity Press, 2008.

Tan, Siang-Yan, and Douglas H. Gregg. *Disciplines of the Holy Spirit: How to Connect with the Spirit's Power and Presence.* Grand Rapids, MI: Zondervan, 1997.

Thomas, Gary. *Sacred Pathways: Discover Your Soul's Path to God*, revised edition. Grand Rapids, MI: Zondervan, 2010.

Thurman, Chris. *The Lies Couples Believe.* Colorado Springs, CO: David C. Cook, 2015.

———. *The Lies We Believe About God.* Colorado Springs, CO: David C. Cook, 2017.

Tozer, A. W. *The Knowledge of the Holy: The Attributes of God; Their Meaning in the Christian Life.* New York: HarperSanFrancisco, 1961.

Welch, Ed. *Shame Interrupted: How God Lifts the Pain of Worthlessness and Rejection.* Greensboro, NC: New Growth Press, 2012.

———. *When People Are Big and God Is Small: Overcoming Peer Pressure, Codependency, and the Fear of Man.* Phillipsburg, NJ: P & R Publishing, 1997.

Willard, Dallas. *Renovation of the Heart: Putting on the Character of Christ.* Colorado Springs, CO: NavPress, 2002.

———. *The Spirit of the Disciplines: Understanding How God Changes Lives.* New York: HarperOne, 1999.

Yancey, Philip. *The Jesus I Never Knew.* Grand Rapids, MI: Zondervan, 1995.

———. *What's So Amazing About Grace?* revised edition. Grand Rapids, MI: Zondervan, 2002.

About the Author

Dr. Chris Thurman is a psychologist who maintains a private counseling practice in Austin, Texas. He earned a Ph.D. in counseling psychology from the University of Texas. Dr. Thurman is a best-selling author and highly sought-after speaker who has conducted hundreds of seminars for churches and corporations around the country. He and his wife, Holly, have three grown children and live in Austin, Texas. For more information concerning Dr. Thurman's seminars, *The Lies We Believe*, *Emotionally Healthy Christianity*, and *Making Marriage Work*, please contact him at drchristhurman.com.

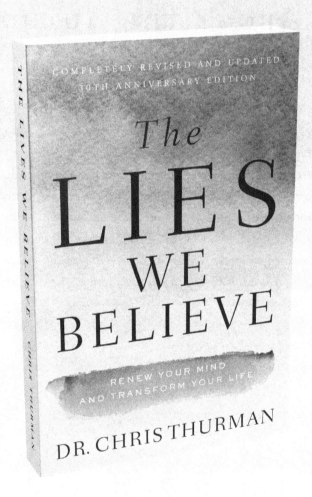

Printed in the USA
CPSIA information can be obtained
at www.ICGtesting.com
JSHW060144120823
46366JS00006B/25